The
Brand
Book

An insider's guide to brand building
for businesses and organizations.

Daryl Fielding

Laurence King

First published in Great Britain in 2022 by

Laurence King Student & Professional
An imprint of Quercus Editions Ltd
Carmelite House
50 Victoria Embankment
London EC4Y 0DZ

An Hachette UK company

A CIP catalogue record for this book is available
from the British Library

PB ISBN 978-1-52942-017-3
E-BOOK ISBN 978-1-52942-018-0

10 9 8 7 6 5 4 3 2

Design by Charlotte Bolton

Printed and bound in China by C&C Offset Printing Co., Ltd.

Papers used by Quercus are from well-managed forests
and other responsible sources.

Contents

Introduction

Why this book?

A brand is a simple concept: the combination of product or service and reputation which creates preference. In other words, it's 'the thing' plus what people think about the thing.

Yet, four months into my job as Brand Marketing Director at Vodafone UK, I realized that my fellow directors did not always distinguish between the terms 'brand' and 'advertising'. I had spent the past ten years of my working life employed in the so-called fast-moving consumer goods sector (FMCG), which comprises mainly products sold in supermarkets, bought regularly and often by consumers. The sector had generally been regarded as the gold standard for marketing capability. I had been responsible for brands, or their advertising, such as Dove, Hellmann's, Cadbury and Milka, and the moment when I realized that the directors of the UK's biggest brand were often not on exactly the same page as me came as a huge shock. Then began my long march to get everyone to understand that 'brand' was a bigger concept than 'advertising'. As I said to Vodafone UK's CFO (chief financial officer): 'Customers spend more time with our bills than with our television commercials. The brand is everything we do.'

Several years on, in the world of marketing the debate still rages, with insults traded between the 'digiterati' and the 'dinosaurs' – the latter insult aimed mainly at those in the consumer goods industry. 'We don't do brands,' cry the digiterati; or 'The dinosaurs just have to die and all will be well in the world when it is fully digital.' 'Digital marketing is just about channels,' retort the executives of 'old school' companies, furious at losing their spot at the top of the marketing food chain, their anger fuelled by insecurity about their own digital competence.

As a marketer who has worked in both classic FMCG and digital businesses, I would like this book to help broker peace between the factions. I hope it re-establishes the building of brands as simply something that adds commercial value to an organization. Any organization. I prefer that to communism and commodity markets.

Who is this book for?

It amazes me that members of the public understand the concept of a brand pretty clearly, yet the majority of marketers don't. Not only is that a scandal for the marketing industry but it also damages commerce. Marketers are not building as much value as they could for the businesses that employ them, and marketing is thereby becoming devalued as a profession.

I'm also staggered by the lack of investment in the training of marketers. Although the explosion of digital businesses over the last two decades has created more people with marketing included in their role, most of those people have very little training and many have none whatsoever. We now have a population of marketers who are, effectively, feral. No wonder businesses are creating new roles such as Chief Customer Officer or Head of User Experience as they seek individuals who can create enhanced customer loyalty and business value. That is what marketers used to do.

So, this book is for everyone. It is a book that the digiterati will have the most to learn from, as they build their careers mostly by understanding performance marketing and data.

Furthermore, they are often working for senior executives who haven't needed to understand brands in the early stages of high growth. When the growth slows or the category reaches maturity, it's then that the organization looks to find ways to grow by innovation and brand building and finds it lacks the skills within the company. I hope digital marketers will enjoy learning about brands from the book and begin to apply what they learn as they grow their CVs. They may find they have unique skills in their organization, and this will benefit their career. The book is also for the underinvested folk in 'traditional' marketing and their agencies who simply aren't taught this stuff anymore. I intend it to be a practical, common-sense guide to defining and building every kind of brand. It is for students of marketing; marketers learning their craft in traditional businesses; entrepreneurs starting or scaling their business; those leading pure-play digital businesses. It is for anyone who is interested in adding value to their organization. I hope it will be illuminating and fun, enlivened by my irreverent spirit that has helped and hindered my career in equal measure.

Part 1: Strategy

Whenever I get called in to advise on brands or marketing, CMOs (chief marketing officers), CEOs (chief executive officers) or business owners immediately want to jump straight to execution. Of course, there may be things that are not working and that need an immediate fix, which is fair enough, but to build a brand and to deliver really effective marketing, you have to start with a strategy. In fact, to do almost anything well, you need a strategy.

What is strategy?

Even personal decisions have a strategy. Consider a group of friends planning to go on holiday. You'd decide who was going with you, how much you were prepared to spend, whether you wanted sun, adventure, culture – wouldn't you? If you all piled in with a random list of potential destinations, sooner or later one of you would interject, 'Hang on a moment, what kind of thing are we actually planning here?' Resolving the discussion between a camping trip to the Alps or a clubbing fest in Ibiza would be a lot easier if you had already decided it was girls only and a chance to unwind, get a tan and enjoy a bit of luxury. Similarly, you wouldn't start a conversation with an architect by asking whether your extension should be a modernist glass box or not. I am amazed how often starting a discussion on brands or marketing without a mention of a strategy happens in business. The CEOs and MDs, especially of smaller organizations, who ask me if they should be spending more on social media or whether they need a new website are doing exactly this. Executing without a strategy.

When I counsel figuring all the strategy stuff upfront, people want to 'move fast and break things', and protest that this initial work will slow them down. Actually, the opposite is true. The beauty of a strategy – working stuff out properly first – is that it saves time and money pretty quickly once you've done it. You won't waste days on frustrating, protracted and subjective arguments, which are often then revisited when a different collection of people are in the room. You won't waste money on things that don't build a consistent picture in the mind of the customer either. Despite first appearances, it makes everything you do more efficient.

Why is it important?

These days the tenure of chief marketing officers in larger organizations is very short. A recent study showed that the median tenure in the USA was just short of three years, less than half that of a typical CEO. Brands are not built that fast in the minds of the public, so if everything changes every time the CMO changes, your brand really is in trouble. Getting a well-thought-through strategy that everyone buys into will make it stick, and the brand will be built consistently in the minds of the public. One of the most effective brand-building advertising campaigns of all time, for Volkswagen in the UK, was: 'If only everything was as reliable as a Volkswagen.' This was due to the head of marketing there, Johnnie Meszaros, whose tenure spanned two decades. While that kind of continuity of personnel rarely happens now, getting a strategy and keeping it is the best thing you can do for a brand. Unilever, one of the best companies in the world at marketing, does not change its strategy for such brands as Dove, Persil, Marmite or Axe every time the person responsible for them changes job. It doesn't happen there – and rightly so. Dove's global positioning as a brand championing real beauty was created in 2004 and is still going strong. The 'Love it or hate it' campaign for UK brand Marmite was created in 1996, and has now entered the English vernacular.

Brands managed by their owners often do very much better at keeping the brand on track, usually because that business and its history just flows in their veins. I worked on Weetabix's advertising when the company was owned by the George family and was always massively impressed by how good Sir Richard George's instinct was on which TV commercials were great and which less good. The ads the owner loved always sold more. But even with smaller owner-managed businesses, setting out some key strategic principles of brand building can really help to amp up what they are currently doing or help them figure out why certain aspects of what they do just seem right.

How does strategy work?

This first half of the book focuses on what you need to think about and how you can build a clear strategy for your brand. It's a how-to guide, with lots of examples. Some I worked on myself, and some I simply admire.

For the more brand-savvy reader, you can refresh your understanding and learn some best practice. If you are a sceptic, I really urge you not to miss out this stage. 'Failing forward fast', 'moving fast and breaking things', or whatever are the fashionable mantras of the day, were never intended to advocate for random chaos and guessing games. With a strategy, you will do everything faster and be able to take bigger risks because you will have some guardrails to guide success.

We didn't just wake up one day and decide to pop bigger

women in our ads for Dove. That campaign was born after 18 months of thinking through what the brand needed to achieve in business terms, what it could credibly stand for, what it should look like, how it was to relate to its customers, and several other aspects of its positioning. It shifted the paradigm of branding, to pioneer the idea of brand purpose, and was the first global brand to create customer engagement on its own website. It is one of the examples I will draw on throughout the book, as I led the development of the advertising and know the inside track.

To me, not having a strategy is like navigating without a map – even if you get there in the end without one, the journey is clearer, faster and more peaceable with one. And you'll still get there if someone else takes over the driving. Even Siri doesn't have an answer to the request: 'Will you take me somewhere?'

CHAPTER 1

What is a brand and why do brands matter?

Some brands go way back. The Bavarian breweries Weihenstephan and Weltenburger, founded in 1040 and 1050 respectively, are disputing the claim to be the world's oldest German monastic beer. Sudo Honke is a Japanese brand of premium sake founded in 1141 and one of the oldest brands and companies in the world. Guangyuyuan is a Chinese herbal remedy dating from 1541 and is still one of the biggest brands in China. Bushmills, a Northern Irish distillery, was granted a licence in 1609; as Colum Egan, the head distiller, says, 'We're not the best because we're the oldest, we're the oldest because we're the best.' Whether you agree with his assessment or not (some prefer a Scottish single malt, me included), more than 400 years in business, *with the same brand*, demands respect. And his brand-centric point that maintaining quality has made that firm sustainable should give pause for thought.

In the UK, in 1706, Twinings tea company was founded; in 1787 it created its logo, which is believed to be the oldest brand mark in continuous use. Berenberg Bank, from Hamburg, Germany, founded in 1590, is the second-oldest lender in the world, while the banking firm that became known as Barclays started trading in 1690 and adopted the name in 1736. The oldest US brand is Caswell-Massey, selling fragrances and toiletries, founded in 1752 and counting George Washington among its early customers. It now operates across 27 states.

Drinks, smells and money. Sustainable businesses for centuries. What's not to like?

The world's most valuable brands

Every year, an organization that specializes in brand analysis, Kantar, publishes its world rankings of the most valuable brands. If you're that way inclined, it makes interesting reading. This survey values brands not only by using the turnover of the company, but also by calculating the contribution made by reputation. In 2019 the following brands comprised the top ten: Amazon, Apple, Google, Microsoft, Visa, Facebook, Alibaba, Tencent, McDonald's, and AT&T – most of these brands newly minted and tech-based. Alibaba and Tencent are Chinese brands in the global top ten, and very new Chinese lifestyle app brands Meitan and Dianping entered the top 100 in 2019. Unsurprisingly, mobile phone companies – the tide floating many of these app-based boats – from almost every major economy appear in the global top 100, including AT&T (USA), Movistar (Spain), Verizon (USA), Orange (France), Vodafone (UK), T-Mobile (Germany) and NTT (Japan).

Playing to country stereotypes, the top 100 also includes German engineering and tech brands SAP, BMW, Mercedes and

Some of the world's oldest brands. Clockwise from top left: Bushmills (1609), Weihenstephan (1040), Weltenberger (1050), Barclays Bank (1690) and Berenberg Bank (1590).

Mobile phone companies from almost every major economy appear in the global top 100.

Siemens, and French fashion and beauty brands Louis Vuitton, Chanel, Hermès and L'Oréal. Here is an example of how countries' reputations are built. Brand France is definitely chic and perhaps the worldwide brands it sells is one reason why.

From the UK, Vodafone, HSBC and Shell are in the global top 100, with Unilever's Dove and Mondelez's Cadbury in the UK top 20. I have direct experience of working with three of these brands – Vodafone, Dove and Cadbury – and all have an international footprint.

Zara and Movistar for Spain and Gucci for Italy are brands in the global top 100. Brands in the Spanish top 30 span a number of categories, but seven of Italy's top 30 brands are in the luxury category, which no doubt also adds to the country's own brand as the home of *la dolce vita*.

Some of the world's biggest, newest brands, clockwise from top left: Apple (1976), Tencent (1998), Amazon (1994), Facebook (2004), TikTok (2016) and Google (1998).

Brands make their producers accountable

A market without brands is a commodity market. Imagine you are buying rusks for your baby, who is being weaned. There are two identical packs sold at the same price. How would you decide which to get? You shrug and buy one of them, but they upset your baby's tummy. Another mother then says her baby is fine, so you want to get the rusks she uses instead. She comes with you to the shop and tells you that her rusks are slightly lighter in colour. You buy those and your baby's tum doesn't get upset.

But next time you try to get them, all the rusks are the same, darker colour. The shopkeeper tells you that the maker of the lighter rusks has gone out of business, because the costs of keeping the ingredients pure made it unprofitable. Because the customer often couldn't tell the difference (not all babies had delicate tummies and a determinedly curious mum), the manufacturer who did not bother to pasteurize the ingredients was now the only one still trading.

It sounds like a fanciful story. But the truth is, not so very long ago, in the USSR, people had very little choice between products. And without a reason to discriminate, where is the incentive for manufacturers – whether state-owned or private – to keep quality high? The standards of hygiene in state-owned mayonnaise factories in the Soviet bloc were so poor that several people died of mayo-related food poisoning every year, most likely from salmonella from the eggs. The Western brands owned by Unilever and Kraft did not suffer from the same problem. (Russians eat a staggering 9 kilograms, or nearly 20 pounds, of mayo per head per year. My hypothesis as to why they eat so much of it is that the basic ingredients they had for decades under communist rule were so execrable that it created this enormous demand for condiments.)

Brands give customers power

In his book *Alchemy* (2019), Rory Sutherland recounts the story of a friend of his, raised in the Eastern bloc, where there were three different state-owned factories making bars of chocolate. When she was a little girl, her mother made her look inside the wrappers and pick out bars with the letter B, coming from a factory whose output was the most delicious chocolate. Factory B! The very start of a little bit of a brand. Helping people choose.

People want choice, they want a basis on which to make that choice, and businesses are better if they are held to account about their products because people know who makes them.

Reputation is a fundamental part of a brand. If a company's reputation is tarnished by its use of sweatshop labour or unethical disposal of unsold goods and, critically, if its customers care about such things, it will start to lose sales. Then it will mend its ways. In 2018, Burberry was exposed burning £28 million of unsold fashion and cosmetic products to prevent them being sold cheaply. The outcry this caused has resulted in the company's seeking other methods to dispose of stock and, perhaps more significantly, to be more focused in targeting its collections so as to reduce the amount of unwanted stock in the first place.

That is the nub of it. That is what brands are for and why they matter. A business that makes a good product and has a good reputation has the best chance of doing well, and the customer will be better off if they know what they are getting, and they can exercise their rights as a customer to buy or not to buy.

We have never had more transparency in or more scrutiny of corporate behaviour. And that is a good thing. That there is room for improvement is clear, but that does not mean that brands are a bad thing. Quite the opposite.

Brands build commercial value

Creating customer preference should add value, but should also be financially sustainable. Owners need to ensure that they offer something the customer values enough to pay more for, and that they can do so at the same or greater profit. If a business does this successfully, they will add financial value to the organization because, ideally, more customers will choose this enhanced version or new product. You might think this goes without saying.... but clearly it doesn't. It is the easiest thing in the world to cut prices to drive growth or to make a cheaper product to increase profits. But if you drive value out of your brand, customers might actually notice and stop buying it (they aren't daft), or you may risk competitors following your lead and driving value out of the whole market. This book does not focus on value engineering or managing a brand's profits and losses. These are important business fundamentals, so please take this aspect as a given when managing a brand.

People want choice, they want a basis on which to make that choice.

Businesses are better if they are held to account about their products because people know who makes them.

'A brand is the sum of the product and its reputation.'

A clear definition of 'brand'

There are more than half a billion results if you type 'definition of brand' into Google Search. For those of you who have not quite the time to sift this cornucopia of wisdom for the perfect definition, let me give you the one that I like.

'A brand is the sum of the product and its reputation.'

Or, more colloquially, 'the thing and what people think about the thing'.

And for product, read service, organization or any entity. I'm going to call any of these things 'the product' from now on to keep matters simple. To me, the product is what people buy, in the broadest sense of that word. It's what you are offering, whatever that is.

The product and reputation are inextricably entwined. Make a bad product and your reputation will suffer. And the reputation you have will drive the kind of products you develop. If you are known for flame grilling, then you will look for more stuff to flame grill. If you are a retailer with a reputation for high-end glamorous fashion, you may expand into homewares, but at the blingier end of the design spectrum.

Once defined in this way, the discourse about brand rises above the unedifying debate that rages in the marketing industry about image advertising versus the measurability of digital. A CEO might be highly antipathetic to brand building if, to her, it is synonymous with spending vast sums on TV commercials. She will, however, care hugely about the company's reputation. And should be willing to invest to build it.

Brands repairing and building their reputation

Facebook had never seen the need to advertise itself much until 2018, when a particularly large scandal about the transfer of customer data together with concerns about the use of its platform for electoral interference and the dissemination of 'fake news' brought Mark Zuckerberg and his company in front of the US Senate and a UK parliamentary select committee. It increased its US ad budget from $50 million in 2017 to $382 million in 2018, including its 'apology' campaign of full pages featuring a letter signed by Mr. Zuckerberg and another campaign to tackle specific aspects that are undermining customer trust. It also launched a 'More Together' campaign, affirming the role

Facebook's 2018 ads sought to repair trust with customers.

Far left: 'Data misuse is not our friend. Facebook is changing. We're introducing more ways to give you control of your data. We've already begun by putting privacy shortcuts at the top of your News Feed, and letting you restrict how apps use your information.'

Left: 'Fake news is not our friend. We're committed to reducing its spread; so we're working with more fact-checkers globally, improving our technology, and giving you background information on the articles in your News Feed.'

of social media to connect people in groups for meaningful experiences. Whether firefighting or building, this most digital of businesses is coming of age and recognizing a need to address its reputation.

In 2017, a senior marketer from Amazon told me that they didn't believe in brand building but invested everything in their product. As far as I was concerned, they were doing both. What kind of product you make (and what you don't) will, without doubt, determine what kind of reputation you have. The simplest explanation of marketing includes the 'four Ps' – product, price, point of sale, and promotion. Product is part of marketing, and marketing isn't just about promotion or communicating with the customer. Marketing and brand building include the product, and the product is the element that is common to both.

Customers are more part of building a brand than ever before

There is a lot of nonsense spouted about brands. Recently there was a widely trumpeted notion that 'the customer owns the brand'. I don't think you'll find they do when there's a product recall! However, this sentiment hints at the degree to which the customer impacts the brand's reputation. This was always true, but now it is true at the epic scale that social media can drive.

Reputation is built more than ever by customers' experience of the product in the new(ish) world of online reviews and social sharing. From Tripadvisor (where hospitality businesses can be made or broken by what the customer thinks) to Airbnb, what the product delivers is significant. The provision of 'Instagrammable' dishes is now a fundamental part of a restaurant's offer. Exactly what is said and what is shared can be influenced by the company itself, even though it may be disseminated by a third party.

Companies are now gaming user reviews, one tactic being to invite customers declaring themselves to be happy in a private survey to post public reviews. Seems sensible – if I ran a restaurant, I might invite happy customers to give us a Tripadvisor review. That feels like common sense. However, I feel uncomfortable about doing this with automated algorithms. Some link high scorers on private satisfaction surveys to a public review site and invite them to repeat their rave review there; anyone who doesn't give the organization a cracking score in private is not linked to the public site. In this way, a distorted proportion of delighted customer reviews is then seen by the public. I don't like it because it is dishonest and eventually, when the public catch on, it will destroy faith in these otherwise worthwhile rating platforms.

Employers and people are brands, too

I spoke at an education conference recently about brands. A secondary-school headmistress stated that she didn't need a brand because her institution didn't have any competition. 'Can your staff go and work anywhere else?' I asked her by way of reply. She was taken aback but had to admit they could. It powerfully made the case for the employer brand. Where reputation drives choice, you have a brand. In this case, it was her organization's reputation as an employer that was critical to the success of her school.

Glassdoor, a site where current and former employees anonymously review companies, gives this aspect importance and transparency. Reputation has always been a factor in where individuals want to work and even in how they behave when they start. It is always gratifying to me to see that Apple and Rentokil have approximately equal, and good, ratings on Glassdoor at the time of writing. I like the fact that the geeks of Silicon Valley and the rat-catchers of the world are equally fulfilled at work.

Personal branding has become a very popular topic in the era of social media. Individuals have, of course, always had a reputation, it's just that now it is possible to build and disseminate

Personal branding has become a very popular topic in the era of social media.

it on a scale that is exponentially larger than in the past. And young people are more aware of their image and take pains to 'curate' it. In careers, personal brand is often discussed, and in bigger companies it is normal to be assessed on 'the how' as well as 'the what'. Your skills and your reputation are obviously important when it comes to building a career. Back to your personal brand being the product and the reputation again.

In conclusion: brands have no right to exist, but it's better that they do

If you find yourself in London, it is fun to wander round the Museum of Brands, in Notting Hill, the only one of its kind in the world. (Most other such museums are devoted to a single brand, and you can visit Hershey's in Pennsylvania, Mazda's in Hiroshima and Gucci's in Florence; for the very devoted, there is even a Spam museum in Minnesota.) Along with others from the Vodafone European senior management team, I was taken to the Museum of Brands as part of a leadership development course. We noted how some brands had changed over the years, including Coca-Cola, which has evolved and modernized throughout its lifetime. But we also noticed many more that weren't around anymore. That was our lesson for the morning: 'Brands have no right to exist'. You have to work at it. You have to invest and evolve. Organizations that neglect this are unlikely to survive four decades, let alone four centuries.

Someone asked me recently why a lot of branding was 'such shit'. My reply was that excellence is hard.

I believe that brands are an essential driver of the capitalist economy. For those who don't like capitalism, there's still Cuba. Brands empower customers and make producers accountable. Brands drive financial success for their owners. Critics often say that brands create aspirations that can't be fulfilled and that this creates unhappiness. They also often imply that people will buy things they don't want or need. My view is that the customer isn't as stupid as the critics make out and that the alternative world without brands is far worse.

So, a brand is the combination of product and reputation. Figuring this out and building it over years, decades and centuries is what follows! Someone asked me recently why a lot of branding was 'such shit'. My reply was that excellence is hard. That's why it's rare. I hope the following chapters help make it a little bit easier for everyone.

CHAPTER 2

Positioning your brand

When people talk about strong brands, they mean brands whose customers have a very strong preference for them. The holy grail for an organization is for their customers to refuse all alternative brands. Try giving a Mac user a PC on their first day in a new job, and you will see exactly what I mean.

Getting to this state is rare: most people will buy something else if they can't get their first choice or if something is on offer or cheaper. Brand owners want to move their customers through a number of stages: awareness, consideration, preference and loyalty.

But before embarking on trying to move the customer from ignorance to obsession, a fundamental matter needs to be figured out first: brand positioning. This covers six main aspects: Which market is the brand in? Who is your brand competing with? How does it sit relative to the competition? Who is it for? What does it offer in particular that's different or better, and why is this true? These need to be considered one by one, but they are all related, and connecting all these dots will have you go round the block several times until the logic of it all falls into place. Deciding how to define your customer is the subject of two whole chapters (see Chapters 4 and 5), so for the purposes of this one, we will assume that has already been figured out and focus on the other aspects of positioning.

The holy grail for an organization is for their customers to refuse all alternative brands.

Which market are you in?

This might seem a very obvious question. We make widgets: we are in the widget market. We are a watch: we are in the watch market. We are an online bookseller: we are in the book market. However, considering this wisely and more broadly for your brand can significantly improve its prospects.

Are premium watchmakers like Audemars Piguet, Breitling, Hublot and many others really in the time-telling market? If they are, they are going to have a hard time justifying why you'd pay tens of thousands of dollars for the privilege of donning one of their watches. They are more likely in the status jewellery or luxury goods market. At the time of writing this, if you go to Watches of Switzerland wanting something to tell a man the time, you can spend £446,400 on a Bovet Recital 22 Grand Recital, £70,800 on an Audemars Piguet Royal Oak Offshore or £5000 on a Breitling Navitimer. Or you could acquire the elegantly simple Tissot T-Classic Everytime for a more accessible £195, the least expensive man's watch on the site.

Customers are clearly paying for something more. Swiss craftsmanship, yes, but also the scarcity of the watch (let's face it, not many people can afford to drop these sums on a watch). Possibly also they are buying a signal it sends about wealth or discernment. As if to prove the very point I am making, I can't actually read the time on the Bovet!

Amazon began life as a seller of books online, but by building its delivery and tech capability and expanding its market, it became the world's biggest online general retailer. It's now broadening into being a technology company, alongside Apple, Google and Facebook, by entering the cloud computing, digital streaming and artificial intelligence (AI) market.

In going for ever bigger markets, you must beware of losing focus or attempting to be all things to all people. If you try to appeal to everyone, you end up appealing to no one. A balance needs to be struck between offering something specific and relevant and attracting the biggest number of customers you can.

If you try to appeal to everyone, you end up appealing to no one.

So maybe 'Which market are you in?' is not such a simple question; but it is a very important one. Once you figure this out, other decisions such as what you offer customers and what you communicate about yourself become easier to decide.

As a way to make this clear, let's imagine you are launching a pizza restaurant in Seatown, a small, wholesome coastal resort – charming but not yet in the trendy league. You want to make wood-fired pizzas at the more gourmet end of the spectrum. You know that your customers are mostly tourists and, in that town, most of the tourists are families with children. There are 22 restaurants open for lunch and dinner in town as follows:

There are five shack-style fish places – the sort you find by beaches and harbours everywhere in the world and which in every town range from the sublime to a national disgrace. In Seatown, we have such establishments from the disgrace end of the range to a posh option where you can feast on locally caught lobsters. There are also three takeout restaurants (Indian, Chinese, pizza), three fine-dining options (French, Italian and seafood), six mid-priced restaurants (a Spaghetti House, a gourmet burger, a Thai, a high-tone seafood eatery, a taco joint and a farm-to-fork steakhouse) and five gastropubs. The first question to ask is: What presents the biggest business opportunity?

If you think you are in the pizza market, you would be trying to take business from one restaurant. If you tried to take customers only from the Italian restaurants, you would be stealing business from three out of 22 establishments. But if you decided you were in the family restaurant market, you could take business from all but the pubs and bars and the restaurants serving spicy foods that many children are not accustomed to. You could then source custom from 14 restaurants. Much bigger and better, yet still not trying to be all things to all people.

How do you sit relative to your competition on price?

To buy your product or service, your customers are going to have to switch their spending to you, so you need to think about what people are choosing instead of your product and why. Where will you take sales from, i.e. what is the 'source of business'? Products rarely create or grow a market, although, of course, there are some notable exceptions that have, such as iTunes or the Sony Walkman. More usual is that you have to take customer dollars from someone else's business, also known as taking market share. Many marketers' bonuses and even careers depend on the taking of market share.

Price is a factor in almost all customer decisions. So, deciding where you sit with regard to price needs to happen irrespective of all the other positioning decisions. When I was at Vodafone, I stated in a UK board meeting that we were a premium brand. My colleagues, whose roles were less brand-centric than mine, were appalled because for 'premium' they heard 'luxury'. Once I explained that all this meant was that we were going to charge a little more than some others in the market, everyone calmed down. Charging a premium for something means you want customers to pay a little more for your product, and for that they will need to have a reason.

There are almost as many reasons to pay a little more as there are brands, but the following might apply:

- Better ingredients or enriched materials.
- Better product performance or service.
- User imagery – used by people the customer aspires to be like.
- Celebrity or expert endorsement. Worn by David Beckham, or 'the toothpaste dentists recommend'.
- Sold only in premium locations.
- More beautiful design.

By contrast, a 'value offer' can be an excellent basis for a strong brand. Not all brands succeed because they charge more. That this is the primary goal of branding is a fallacy. The primary goal of branding is to give customers a reason to choose. And low prices might be that reason. There are many brands that have made this their raison d'être, such as Walmart, Aldi, Skoda and Primark. Miniso, a Chinese low-cost retailer of cosmetics, stationery, toys and kitchenware, entered the Chinese market pretending to be Japanese in 2013 and now has more than 1,600 stores across six continents, growing from a predominantly Asian footprint; it even has a store in North Korea. It opened its first UK store in 2019 in Ealing, London, presenting itself as Japanese. I think most companies would be more than happy with the business performance of all these firms.

A value offer can be an excellent basis for a strong brand.

The big risk is that a 'low prices' positioning is easy to copy and, if the whole market follows suit, can drive profit out of an entire market or even eliminate it. German food retailing is an example of a market that ruined itself with a headlong dash to the bottom. Discounters such as Aldi and Lidl convinced one of the richest nations on earth that food should be cheap. I have found shopping for groceries in supermarkets Germany a depressing experience, with many goods displayed in cardboard boxes on the floor and no 'theatre' as there is in the UK or the USA. The British printed newspaper market is another example of a market that drove itself almost to extinction by discounting and giveaways rather than brand building. Once everyone is at the bottom, how do you compete? That's a hard one to figure out!

How do you sit relative to your competition on aspects that drive customer choice?

Understanding what your customer considers when they choose in your category and how they pick between you and your competitors is key to figuring out your market positioning. Price may or may not be one of the key drivers, but it often is.

Companies often map how the customer relates to the market in four quadrants, with the two axes related to key drivers of customer preference. And then they put themselves and the competition on the map. If you owned the pizzeria in Seatown, you would have chatted to families on holiday there and established that price and family suitability were the key factors in deciding where to eat. You know you want to have a premium offer, and you can quickly figure out who your competition are. And you can then go on to figure out what they don't have and how you can appeal even more strongly to those families.

What are you going to offer the customer and why is it true?

The offer needs to be two things: relevant and differentiated. If you know your customer and you know what they could choose instead of you, it ought to be possible to figure out what you can offer that is something they want (relevant), and what you can do better – ideally, something no other competitor can do at all (differentiated).

I am amazed that in many B2B (business-to-business) markets all the companies seem to offer the same thing. Ironically, the advertising agency industry is one of the most undifferentiated markets I have had the misfortune to analyze. It is also oversupplied. And then advertising agencies wonder why clients are cutting their fees. They honestly ought to know better.

Getting back to the pizzeria, it is clear that you are going to take customers from the family restaurants in the town. Your research tells you that other premium offerings are doing well, so this is a sense check on your desire to provide a better class of pizza. Your competitors are 7 Bone Burger, The Inn on the Beach, The Fish Plaice, Pier Head and La Trattoria.

But why would your customers want to come? Why would they choose you in preference to the other options?

Having chatted with a few families on holiday, you realize that eating out with children is a minefield and keeping everyone happy is a challenge of paramount importance. A perfect meal out is when everyone likes what they are eating (kids are really picky and food preferences and allergies are becoming a real challenge) and when for the kids there is something else to do other than eat. If the kids are happy, the adults are happy. And a big glass of wine won't hurt either! For the parents, of course.

Everyone likes pizza, and a big variety on the menu can help, but is that really going to give you the edge? You think a bit harder about what you could do even better than the other restaurants and decide that pizzas are easy to customize. Everyone could even order on an iPad with a gamified app and the pizza would be served with a flag with their name on it.

And it would be easy to let kids watch their own pizza being made, adding their final topping themselves if they wanted. This would be difficult for the other restaurants to copy – their

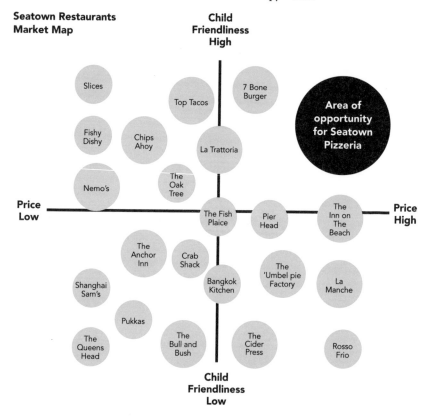

Seatown Restaurants Market Map

Child Friendliness High

Slices

Top Tacos

7 Bone Burger

Area of opportunity for Seatown Pizzeria

Fishy Dishy

Chips Ahoy

La Trattoria

Nemo's

The Oak Tree

Price Low

The Fish Plaice

Pier Head

The Inn on The Beach

Price High

The Anchor Inn

Crab Shack

The 'Umbel pie Factory

La Manche

Shanghai Sam's

Bangkok Kitchen

Pukkas

The Queens Head

The Bull and Bush

The Cider Press

Rosso Frio

Child Friendliness Low

kitchens are already in situ, while you can design yours to accommodate this customer involvement. You have a thing called an 'ownable point of difference'! Who knew?

You decide to name it 'Pizza United' because this embodies what you will be offering. And other decisions will flow from the strategy. This is just one example of what the second half of the book is about – executing a strategy.

Empty promises generally go down badly with customers (strangely obvious if you simply think of them as human beings!). Any offer to customers should be capable of substantiation, and this is often known in marketing circles as 'the reason(s) to believe'. In the case of Pizza United, the claim that they are the ideal choice for families on holiday is substantiated by the pizza offering (everyone loves pizza) as well as them being customizable via a gamified iPad and the entertainment value

Market map for the luxury automotive sector

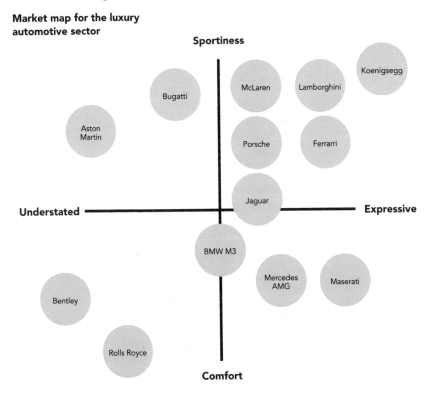

of kids being allowed to watching the pizza being made.

If you offer something that is not delivered, customers these days will trash you on review sites and social media, and more than ever it's not the recipe for a successful business. And, in some countries, it's against the law.

Reasons to believe are not always logical or rational and that's because people, aka customers, aren't either. Believing that David Beckham uses a certain aftershave, for instance, gives a reason to choose, even though in your heart of hearts you know that the brand using him was probably the one with the biggest chequebook.

If you offer something that is not delivered, customers these days will trash you on review sites and social media.

Lucozade's repositioning over the years.

Repositioning

Moving the brand from one market to another or from one target customer to another is known as repositioning it. Many brands choose to do this when sales begin to plateau and they need to look for ways to grow.

One of the classic examples of entering a different market is that of a drink called Lucozade in the UK. In the 1950s and '60s it was a carbonated glucose drink you had when you were ill. 'Lucozade aids recovery' was the slogan. In the 1980s, the company decided to move from the sickness market to being about refreshment and sport, with a commercial featuring decathlete Daley Thompson. During the next few decades they created the sports drink category, launching a large product range and in 2015 they moved on again, beyond sport to overall wellbeing, with the 'Find your Flow' campaign.

Figuring out your positioning statement

Most companies turn this work on positioning into a short and clear statement that connects all these aspects together.

Our Seatown pizzeria's statement could go something like this:

'Pizza United is a premium pizza restaurant, ideal for families with children enjoying a holiday in Seatown because our high-quality wood-fired pizzas with customizable toppings, and the opportunity for kids to watch and help their pizzas being made, ensure each individual is likely to be able to get their favourite and have fun creating it.'

It's not very poetic, but it is crystal clear. Positionings aren't what you say to your customers but are for internal purposes, where strategic clarity matters because it helps management make decisions on what to do and what not to do. And it helps if it's so short and sweet that managers can remember it and don't have to reach for a manual every time they need to decide things. If this does not exist or is not fully embraced by the organization, it is incredible how much time is wasted in debate and rework. Clear strategies make companies efficient.

Clear strategies make companies efficient.

This all may seem little more than common sense. I'm amazed how many small businesses I speak to (and some of the big ones, too!) don't figure out this very basic logic, whether or not they know that it's called brand positioning.

Common sense seems not to be as common as often supposed.

Airbnb

For individuals who seek authentic travel experiences, Airbnb is the accommodation website that enables them to live like a local by connecting them with local hosts.

IKEA

For everyone to whom their home matters, IKEA is a manufacturer and retailer of home furnishing products which democratizes a better everyday life by offering a wide range of well-designed, functional products at prices so low that as many people as possible will be able to afford them.

Mailchimp

For small businesses with customers around the world, Mailchimp is an all-in-one marketing platform that empowers customers to start and grow their businesses with our smart marketing technology, award-winning support and inspiring content.

Chanel

For discerning individuals with understated yet creative taste, Chanel creates luxury products enabling wearers to demonstrate their 'savoir faire' because of its devotion to exceptional creations, ultimate luxury and the highest level of craftsmanship.

CHAPTER 3

Ways to devise your strategy

Companies often use frameworks to help them devise brand strategy. Huge multi-brand companies, where staff will move from brand to brand throughout their career, tend to have a consistent way of doing things, not only to engender best practice but also so individuals don't have to adapt to different ways of working whenever they move jobs.

When Kraft Foods bought Cadbury in 2010, I was the Vice President of Marketing Europe, overseeing the marketing integration, among other things. The marketing teams from each company spoke totally different languages on the topic of brands, which, combined with the fears and resentments on both sides arising from the takeover, made the integration even harder. We had to bring both teams together and get them using a common framework and language. Instead of picking one existing framework over the other, we used this as an opportunity to upgrade and create a world-class new system. Led by the spectacularly brainy and obscenely funny global VP, Dana Anderson, we created a way of figuring out a brand strategy which I have not seen bettered. This chapter simplifies this thinking and some examples that resulted from it.

Other companies have different frameworks and I include some examples of these as well. Most frameworks have a shape that becomes the name of the branding system. They are called things from 'brand keys' to 'brand pyramids' to 'brand houses'; 'brand umbrellas' to the weirder 'brand onions'. All contain a series of factors that drive towards a single big thought that encapsulates what the brand is all about. Kraft's system was called 'four box' – odd, as there are actually five boxes, but arguably better than having an onion. To be frank, these frameworks could be brand dodecahedrons – it's not really the shape of the framework that matters, it's having structured thinking and what you populate it with that drives excellence. And, like most corporate systems, it unites marketing teams across a company.

If you Google 'brand strategy frameworks', you will get around 41 million results. This chapter features a couple you'll be most likely to come across and one or two others that I think are good. Most contain the same basic elements. You pays your money and you chooses your shape.

The brand pyramid or brand benefit ladder

These are two of the most commonly encountered frameworks and the ones still taught in many educational establishments and textbooks. They start with the functional features of the product and build to the functional benefits, to emotional benefits, to personality and to a brand idea. They are essentially two different metaphors for the same thinking, beginning with the product and logically building upwards to the benefits to the customer. As they go from base to peak, pyramids often build to benefits that are more emotional or spiritual, but essentially the frameworks are interchangeable.

The brand benefit ladder is straightforward and widely understood in marketing communities. However, in my opinion, it lacks sufficient focus on the competition, on what makes your brand different, and does not acknowledge the wider context in which the brand operates. Its origins are a bit misty, but it was probably developed in the middle of the 20th century, an era well before the fast-paced copycat culture of today's supply chains, the intensity of competition and the curse and opportunity of social media's ability to impact reputation.

You could, of course, consider differentiation and context filling out these frameworks, but I prefer to be explicit about these factors in defining a brand strategy. These are nice and simple frameworks, understood by many, and on these pages we show some indicative examples, interpreted by me.

Brand Benefit Ladder*

	FRAMEWORK	GATORADE
How does that make me feel?	Emotional Benefit	Makes me feel I have a competitive advantage and feel like a winner
What does the customer get as a result?	Customer Benefit	Enables me to play harder for longer
What the product does	Product Benefit	Replenishes minerals and fluids
Most distinguishable features of the product	Product Features	7% electrolyte formulation. Endorsed by sporting organizations.

Brand Pyramid for Facebook*

FACEBOOK

Brand Essence	The high-level thought that sums up the brand	**Bring the world closer**
Brand Beliefs, Values or Persona	Manifestations of the brand in human terms	**The innocent archetype**
Emotional Benefit	How does this make the customer feel?	**At the centre of their universe**
Customer Benefit	What does the customer get?	**The power to build community**
Features and Attributes	Most distinctive and relevant aspects of the product	**A social network connecting people with friends and others across the globe**

*Indicative example interpreted by author from publicly available information

Some frameworks have evolved the pyramid and based it on Maslow's hierarchy of needs, and the pinnacle becomes a more purpose-oriented self-expression benefit. Here is an example, together with an illustration done for Airbnb.

There is a risk with this laddering or pyramid system that the pinnacle becomes so far removed from the product offer as to be ridiculous. Not only can the resultant brand claims be risible, but they can also result in what I call 'And so and so and so' communications. You can ladder up from a toilet cleaner to world peace, but in trying to explain why LavO is saving humankind, so many leaps of logic are required that the communications become monstrously convoluted.

There is a risk with this laddering or pyramid system that the pinnacle becomes so far removed from the product offer as to be ridiculous.

Maslow's Hierarchy applied to Airbnb*

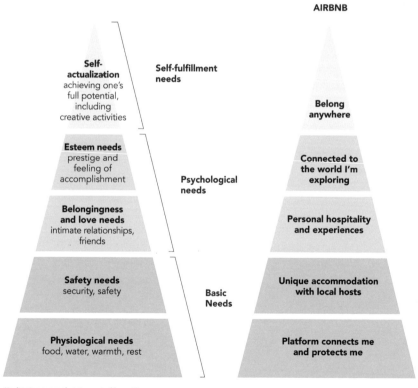

*Indicative example interpreted by author

LavO…too laddered up gives rise to convoluted or ludicrous logic.

Going too far with the laddering up

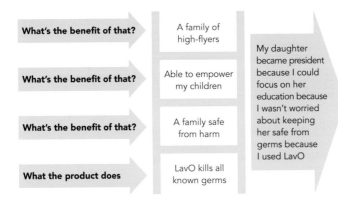

What's the benefit of that?	A family of high-flyers		
What's the benefit of that?	Able to empower my children	My daughter became president because I could focus on her education because I wasn't worried about keeping her safe from germs because I used LavO	My daughter became president because I used LavO
What's the benefit of that?	A family safe from harm		
What the product does	LavO kills all known germs		

The brand key

Unilever is one of the foremost brand builders in the world, and for many years used a model called the 'brand key' to define its brands, comprising eight elements: the competitive environment, target audience, insight, benefits, values or personality, reasons to believe, the discriminator and finally, the Brand Essence, which draws all this together.

Although this covers all the key elements that should be reviewed in defining a brand, I find it a little hard to remember. I prefer a more succinct distillation, as it helps marketing teams recall it without getting a document out – not very practical in your everyday working life. It is much more competition- and differentiation-driven than the pyramid or benefit ladder, but still overlooks the context, which is more important than ever in that it shapes customer opinion and enables brands to join in and connect with customers in social media more readily.

The brand house

This framework features a roof with pillars and sometimes also has a foundation underpinning it. Typically, the roof will feature the overarching thought about the brand, and the pillars are the key elements informing that, usually the market, the product and its benefits, and the customer. Houses are common strategic frameworks across many functions and organizations, so it has the advantage of familiarity to all.

The Brand House

BRAND VISION
What the brand is to be or to stand for

BRAND AMBITION
Longer-term sales target/organizational objective
and change in brand needed and by when.

MARKET	BRAND	PEOPLE
Category What category is the brand and what could the brand's impact be on it? **Competition** Who are the brand's generic competitors, in or out of our immediate category, and what does ours have that can beat them?	**Highest order benefit** What does the brand offer customers? **Emotional benefit** What does the brand offer customers? **Product features and benefits** What does the brand offer customers?	**Customer context** What is going on in the world that impacts our customer and that is relevant to our brand? **Target customer** Who are we going to gain business from or seek to influence? Key insights into their needs and wants and drivers.

Example of the brand house for Coca Cola, deduced by the author from publicly available information

BRAND VISION
Become the world's happiness icon.
Around the world, 1.5 billion times every day

BRAND AMBITION
Brand: re-establish Coca Cola's ownership of happiness.
Business: Drive recruitment into the wider brand franchise.

MARKET	BRAND	PEOPLE
Category Niche and healthier brands are depositioning us amid misperceptions about sugar, caffeine and empty calories. We need to reassert the positive functional and emotional benefits of the category and our ownership of them. **Competition** A broad range of brands are entering the happiness business – despite our ownership of optimism for the past century. We compete daily for share of hearts and minds across this broad base.	**Highest order benefit** Highest order benefit Optimism **Emotional benefit** Uplifting moments every day **Product features and benefits** Great taste, refreshment, uplift. Mythology, connectedness, cultural leadership.	**Customer context** The daily challenges of life today are increasing people's desire for authentic happiness. They seek small acts that can lead to big things and to reframe the world in a more positive way, knowing there are plenty of reasons to be happy. **Target customer** The popular mainstream of wishful wannabes who have within them a live-for-now spirit, and the capacity to believe and to dream.

Coca-Cola have a good one for all their brands, with the 'brand vision' forming the roof supported by three pillars, underpinned by the foundation of 'ambition', which articulates the longer-term business objectives and the objectives for the brand (see opposite).

The golden circle

This is my second-favourite framework, because it is very clear and enables brands to stand for something bigger than their products. I have used it when consulting and find it especially helpful for start-ups. The system was invented by Simon Sinek, who presented it in 2009 in a book, *Start with Why*, and the golden circle has become a common tool for brand strategists. It looks at the what, the how and the why. Sinek's argument as to how his system works is that the 'what' part activates your neocortex or rational brain, while the 'how and why' activates your brain's limbic system – responsible for feelings such as trust and loyalty, often known as 'gut feelings'.

Activating both these parts of the brain enables leaders to inspire the members of their organizations, and brands to motivate their consumers. Sinek also believes that starting the conversation with 'Why' is a powerful way to communicate.

The 'what' in the golden circle states what products they sell or the service they offer; the 'how' articulates the things that make them special or that set them apart from the competition. The all important 'why' defines the organization's purpose, cause or belief; the reason the organization exists apart from making money. I used to ask my clients to answer the question 'Why is your brand on the planet?' For some reason phrasing it like this, tends to get to a deeper reason.

Sinek often illustrates his framework by using an imaginary example for Apple, which goes as follows:

'Why: Everything we do, we believe in challenging the status quo, we believe in thinking differently.

How: We make products that are beautifully designed and user-friendly.

What: We just happen to make great computers, wanna buy some?'

It is a convincing schtick and a great example to illustrate his thinking but in reality, Apple don't use this framework for their brand!

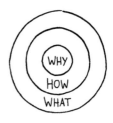

Simon Sinek's Golden Circle (looking at the what, the how and the why) has become a common tool for brand strategists.

The four levers model

This is my own evolution of the framework we developed at Kraft Foods, now Mondelez. It includes customer insight and product offer, like almost all brand strategies, but it includes equal emphasis on why your brand is different and the relevant context for the brand. I believe that differentiation and context create a better framework, as these factors are crucially important in today's hyper-connected and hyper-competitive markets. The inputs/ levers connect together to define a core message, thought, idea or theme that the brand will stand for. You then write this up as a manifesto, a longer and more poetic version of the theme.

So, four levers, a theme and a manifesto. Simple to say, but as with all frameworks, it's hard to deliver the content well. And with all these, brevity helps, and that is also hard.

I also like this framework because its form demands better balance and direct connection between all the key elements. The ladder and pyramid might beat it on logic, but in my view those systems tend to be one-dimensional and excessively rational because they derive from product performance, with less emphasis on customer feelings. Brands are emotional things – and so are customers.

Furthermore, when the brand theme is executed it has more scope to connect directly with all the four inputs. It easily ranges from explaining a new product to engaging in social media conversations without struggling to connect those things with the brand's theme.

Brands are emotional things – and so are customers.

It also links directly with the product offer, which is often a deficit with the ladder or pyramid. You should be able to link the brand idea with 'because' to what the product offers.

For example:

- Vodafone supports your bolder life because you can depend on its stronger network.
- Milka awakens your sweet nature because its melty chocolate makes you feel happier.
- Dove's beauty is honest because we don't show retouched models but real women as they really are.

When it comes to executing the strategy, the inputs become levers for the brand and can be operated to different degrees at different times. Which to operate and when is highlighted later in the book and there are chapters on each aspect of this model with fuller explanations and examples. As we are comparing and contrasting frameworks here, what follows is a summary of the four levers model.

The four levers model in more detail

There are four elements that form the first stage of figuring out a brand using this model:

1. Customer insight. The best practice here is when the insight derives from the customer relationship with the category in which the brand operates. And the insight comes from deep heart, soul and gut stuff, not shallow insights based on surface behaviour. This is examined in more depth in Chapters 4 and 5.

2. Right to win. This is what you have to offer that is particular to you and relevant to the customer. Once upon a time, it might have been known as the USP, or unique selling proposition, but these days nothing stays unique for long, so I think it's best not to delude yourself on this point. This answers the question: What right does your product or service have to succeed with the customer versus other things they might choose?

3. Differentiation. This describes the main way that the brand is different from the competition. This might be in the benefit offered or how the brand goes about things. It's more likely to be the latter, as most competitors offer the same 'what' these days.

4. Context. What is going on in the world that is relevant to the brand and which has an impact on our customer? There may be more than one possibility to choose from here, and it's a question of testing options against these criteria and selecting the one that you feel is best. It's important that this is a longer-term cultural trend and not a fad. To verify, check the growth and scale of the trend and use your judgement.

Once these aspects have been explored, you need to connect them all together into one overarching idea or theme for the brand. Some may connect more directly than others, but that connection needs to be clear, otherwise the strategy will fall apart when executed or not be effective with customers. This, then, is the brand theme. In other models this is the roof of the house, the essence or the pinnacle of the pyramid, the top rung of the ladder or 'the why'.

Next you write a more poetic expression of the brand theme: the manifesto, a long-form narrative that brings it to life. You don't

need to feature all the levers as a matter of course, only if they help to illustrate a richer version of the brand idea. Some insights are not always nice because the customer's real motivation might be dark or needy. So maybe leave those out. The manifesto is not intended to be shown to the customer, although versions of it often are. It is meant to inspire the staff of the brand-owning organization, especially its marketers, and to make the thinking and strategy memorable. Manifestos are often produced for brands whatever the framework used, more often with those that are richer than the benefit ladder types. Other frameworks do not mandate them, and I think the four levers framework is the better for doing so.

> **Some insights are not always nice because the customer's real motivation might be dark or needy. So maybe leave those out.**

Examples of the four levers model

I am going to show two examples: Dove as retrofitted to this framework, and a reworked example of the model I did at Vodafone. This strategy inspired the staff, and advertising based upon it had begun to work with customers. The ads celebrated Vodafone's customers and gave meaning to the brand's long-running slogan, 'Power to You', which they had used since 2009. After my departure, there was an ad campaign featuring Martin Freeman, concluded both by 'Power to You' and a new end line, launched in 2017: 'The future is exciting. Ready?' Vodafone then replaced this with 'Together we can' in 2021. Vodafone's advertising executions have changed even more often than the tag lines, and I believe that switching so frequently misses an opportunity to build a brand whose heritage, staff and product offer are outstanding.

Vodafone **Dove**

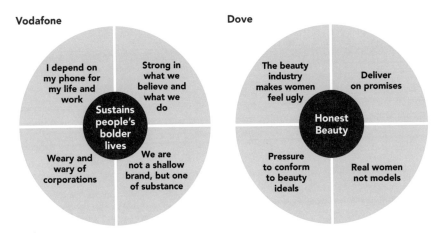

And finally

Whatever framework you prefer, the key thing is that you use something to distil your thinking about the brand. It is important that this is done well, but just as important that it is widely disseminated in the organization and sticks for at least a couple of years. Getting senior buy-in is crucial to enable this to happen, and the topmost brass, including business owners, CEO and board, have to be fully bought into it. The framework has to live outside the marketing department, as the brand should influence everything the organization does. It therefore needs to be widely socialized and, in a big company, even with normal staff turnover, this is a continuous endeavour. Staff also need to understand how they can deliver it in their function. For example, it should influence how front-line colleagues behave towards the customers, what kind of the new products are developed, what the app and websites do and how they look and feel, what kind of hold music you have when customers call in. The list is long: brand impacts everything.

> The framework has to live outside the marketing department, as the brand should influence everything the organization does.

When the brand strategy is revisited, it should not change too much, and the reasons for change should not be because the marketing director has changed but because the customer, the competition or the context has changed or there is a significant change to the product or service offer. Or the execution of the strategy is not delivering results and proper analysis has found that it's the strategy and not the execution that is to blame. In other words, proper reasons, not whims or vanity.

CHAPTER 4

Who are your customers and what do they do?

Any organization will have people it seeks to influence. Whether they are people who buy things from you, use your services or engage with your organization in any other way, I will now for the sake of simplicity call all stakeholders 'the customer'. Even where a monopoly exists, there are customers who may be obliged to use the service or product (schools or the local transport provider spring to mind), and that monopoly may choose to influence its customers' attitudes or behaviour in a way that benefits it. For instance, TfL, the operator of the London Underground, regularly runs ads inviting its passengers to refrain from abusing its staff.

You can define your customer not only by who they are, but by what they do – for example mums, who buy sweets for their children every week; young professionals who exercise every day; families who take short breaks as well as their annual holiday; fleet managers who review their company's automotive suppliers every two years; teenage gamers who play between five and ten different games every month; board chairs who replace one non-executive director every year. The data can also tell you how many of these individuals exist, often country by country, enabling very clear understanding of the business potential.

Whoever you wish to influence as an organization, knowing who they are, what they do when it comes to engaging with you and what is in their minds and hearts is key to success. For almost every brand or marketing task, I always recommend starting with the customer. And being clear on who your brand is for, what they do and what they are like, is important in defining and keeping that brand relevant. Customers do change over time, and, if your brand is to endure, this understanding needs to be refreshed regularly. Any brand or organization that does not have the customer front and centre of its thinking and effort is unlikely to last.

Companies are often tempted to try to appeal to everyone. If you try to be all things to all people, you will end up being nothing to anyone. Strategy is all about choices, and finding out who is your customer (and who isn't), or who you would like them to be in future, is one of the most important choices you will make. Lack of focus rarely delivers success.

In *How Brands Grow* (2010), leading marketing academic and empiricist Byron Sharp reveals that brands grow by acquiring more customers. Actually, this isn't as 'No shit, Sherlock' as it sounds. Brands often believe they can grow by increasing the frequency of use or purchase. Sharp's empirical research has shown that frequency doesn't vary by much. Looking at the top ten brands in a category, the frequency of use of the most popular is only about half as much again as the least popular – yet the most popular brand typically has more than ten times the sales. So the key to growth is more customers and you need to find them either from scratch if you are a new brand, or outside your current customer base. And brands that are lucky enough to be in direct contact with their customers, as many digital brands are, need to know that the biggest scope for increasing business comes from without, not within, their customer base.

The most popular brand typically has only about half again as much frequency of use as the least popular brand, but has ten times the sales.

Brand owners need to know who their customers are in general, where they are, what they do, what they think, how many of them there are now and how many there could be. That understanding will be the key to your brand's success. This chapter focuses on understanding the 'who and what' of customers, and the next chapter on the 'why'.

The challenge with 'big data' is there is often so much information that it can be difficult to extract meaning or insights that can be acted upon.

Being data-driven

Big consumer brands have for decades defined their customer by aspects that can be measured – by methods known collectively as quantitative research. This takes many forms. Traditional data, for example, includes standard demographic data (the social statistics of the population), national consumption, behaviour or shopping surveys, or the company's own bespoke research. Of course, data-driven marketing has massively come of age in the digital era, but digital marketers didn't invent it, even if they invented the term! Companies have been data-driven, if they are sensible, for decades. We now live in the era of 'big data', where data is easier to access and greatly enriched by the arrival of such tools as Google Analytics, social media engagement statistics and the ability to track what the customer does on your own websites. The challenge with 'big data' is there is often so much information that it can be difficult to extract meaning or insights that can be acted upon.

What follows is a review of the most commonly used data to identify customers. It is by no means comprehensive. I have also not chosen the forms of research more commonly used for marketing activity, such as media consumption habits, shopper marketing research and digital econometrics such as last-click attribution modelling. (I bet that's a relief!) As this is a book about brands and not marketing, I have chosen the research forms that are more commonly used for defining brands and figuring out how to innovate. Approaches used to develop products are covered in Chapter 16.

If you are a small business, you might not have access to this sort of research or data, but most businesses are capable of conducting a survey of their existing customers to find more out about them and to do this at a scale that is likely to be statistically robust. Whether this is with a clipboard in store, by email or over the phone – it can be done. And in my view, it should be done. I am amazed at how many smaller firms I have chatted to or consulted with just don't do this.

Customer segmentation

When you analyze your customers in this way, the population can often be defined in clusters or segments. And organizations with more than one brand can decide to target different customer segments with different brands or sub-brands. This is called customer segmentation, and which way you decide to classify your customers depends on whether customers are more or less likely to choose your brand across the segments. For example, if you looked at age as a significant determinant

Knowing your customer from a quantitative point of view also helps with assessing the scope for growth.

of brand usage, it won't be helpful if individuals between 18 and 25 are only 2 per cent more likely to choose your brand than people over 60. It would be better to find some other characteristic that differentiates them.

Knowing your customer from a quantitative point of view also helps with assessing the scope for growth. You may know that that your brand appeals strongly to young men aged 18 to 25 and that you have 100,000 of these customers at present. If you also knew that there were 3 million of them in this age group in the country and that this segment of the population was forecast to grow in the next 20 years, you would be encouraged that there was sustainable headroom to grow. But if you already sold to a significant number of this age group, and it was shrinking, you might choose to widen the appeal of your brand to a slightly older or younger group. Or assess the potential appeal of a female variant.

Demographics

Demographics are the statistics that most developed economies collect about their population, which they mostly acquire from censuses. This is often very similar (though not always identical) to research done by commercial organizations on purchasing behaviour, readership and viewership of media channels and a myriad of other aspects. Demographics typically include gender, age, marital status, presence of children, social class, educational level, working status, and location. Some of these probably don't need much additional comment from me, but I think two are worth further consideration.

Location

At a country level, location is generally collected by governmental districts or regions where TV stations broadcast. In China there are 34 provincial-level administrative regions, with additional categories for military personnel and those whose permanent residence is difficult to define. Any stats related to China tend to blow the minds of most people from other countries because of the huge scale. In 2010, 4.6 million people fell into the 'no fixed abode category' – roughly the population of Ireland – and more than 104 million people reside in the province of Guangdong. In China, most marketing is done on a city-by-city basis, with urbanization being a major trend in the demography of the nation. In 1980, just 18 per cent of Chinese lived in cities; by 2017 it was 58 per cent, or approximately 810 million people. In the USA, the UK and numerous other countries, every residence has a zipcode or a postcode, which research firms combine with other research to classify similar kinds of people in similar neighbourhoods.

Of course, smaller businesses need to figure this out on a case-by-case basis. Will people in the town or in the wider county buy your product or use your service? Do your customers travel to you and, if so, where are they most likely to come from? The market for weekend breaks in country hotels is likely to be from the nearest city, for example. If you are a business-to-business brand, is location a factor at all? It might be if you are targeting Silicon Valley or a manufacturing centre in Guangzhou, less so if you want to attract accountants or lawyers, who lurk pretty much everywhere. And digital businesses are boundaryless unless a physical delivery is required. Location is more likely to be determined by the law of the land where organizations wish to operate than by any other factor.

Affluence

Brands need to know who is likely to be able to afford their products, wealth being another demographic indicator. Most countries are straightforward about this and simply collect income data.

In the USA, data is collected by the government census bureau and the leading independent market data organization, PEW. Educational attainment is also a factor in market research to define customers in the USA, with college degrees being the main factor.

In China, the matter is more straightforward, with most research organizations, including the Chinese government, using income to classify people, although what the state and consultants McKinsey define as middle income is pretty divergent! (The government sets the middle-income earning cap at 500,000 yuan per year, but McKinsey would almost halve this at 280,000 yuan, or $43,000.)

The UK is a notable exception regarding demographics and, sadly, is still a society that defines itself by the notion of 'class'. Almost all surveys there, including the pervasive National Readership Survey (an analysis of media consumption habits) and data collected by the government's Office for National Statistics, distinguish six social classes, based principally on occupation and described alphabetically. A is 'upper middle class', with individuals working in higher managerial, administrative or professional occupations. The occupations within the category have divergent pay grades, although the level of educational attainment and attitudes are likely to be quite similar. Moving on through the alphabet and getting progressively poorer, there follow B, C1, C2, D and E. The cohorts are not of equal size: for example, As comprise just 4 per cent of the population, C1s 28 per cent, C2s 20 per cent and Es 10 per cent. When using these definitions, often the groups are clustered: ABC1 being generally 'upmarket', C2DE being broadly 'working class'. C1C2 is a fairly frequently used grouping as well, indicating a slap-bang-in-the-middle, mass-market customer.

The assumption that wealthier people buy the more expensive products cannot be taken for granted in any market. It is likely to be true, but there are many fascinating exceptions and trends. Buying a new car in the UK is a more downmarket activity than buying a cheaper dealer-registered model, for example. (Dealers commonly register themselves as new owners of a new vehicle, to then sell it at a lower price because, it has had one owner ... the dealer! This takes out the depreciation from the purchase for the real buyer.) Senior citizens in the UK, in the

Examples of customer research and providers.

Definition	Information gained	Source of data
Demographic	Gender, age, class, marital status, social status, income band, location	Government statistics and Census data
Consumption behaviour	Who buys or uses what and what media do they watch	Nielsen, Kantar, Ipsos GfK, IRI and Intage Group plus specialists by industry sector
Browsing behaviour	What websites and digital platforms people visit	Google Analytics. Platform owners, such as Facebook, TikTok, Twitter, Instagram, Snapchat. Gartner. Comscore.

most 'downmarket' classification, are likely to buy at upmarket food retailer Marks & Spencer, because it is a strong stockist of single-serve items. And the global trend for teenagers and young adults to buy clothing from ultra-high-premium brands such as Canada Goose jackets and Balenciaga or Golden Goose trainers blows my baby boomer marketer's mind. Maybe it's a geese thing.

The following is an example of a customer definition based on demographics:

> BMW 5 Series in the UK: AB men, 35–55, married with children, biased towards the southeast of England.

Knowing this, your brand would ensure that it had subtle status cues, would come in masculine colours and would have family-friendly accessories available, such as child seats. Your dealer network would be southern biased, and the location would tell you that the customer was likely to be commuting to London by car. This isn't too bad a start for a brand, and a good marketer could probably develop something decent (if not exceptional) with just this information and a dash of intuition.

Behaviour: commissioned research

Data about customer behaviour is often readily available to larger organizations, and even the smallest companies will have information about what their customers do which can help them define or refine their brand. It's no surprise that customers buy more ice cream when the sun is shining. And, therefore, no surprise that there is a brand of ice cream called Solero. There are large global research companies that collect and syndicate data on customer behaviour. Such syndicated surveys will measure in more detail who is buying any brands and they are a valuable source of competitor data. These surveys measure what is happening in stores as well as home consumption. Methods used to gather this information include using EPOS (electronic point of sale) data, asking customers what they do in telephone or door-to-door surveys, auditing what is in their trash – and everything in between!

Many companies do their own research by interviewing customers about their behaviour, and such research is easy to conduct and relatively cheap, depending on the scale. It can range from recruiting a consistent panel of people who agree to be interviewed or complete surveys on a regular basis to a simple email questionnaire mailed to your customer database. And it's easy and inexpensive to design customer surveys with products now available to the general public, such as SurveyMonkey.

The risk with asking customers themselves what they do is that claimed behaviour is often quite different from actual behaviour, so there is always a bit of a health warning with information gained in this way. Customers often simply don't recall what they actually do or believe that their behaviour is rather better than it is. Anyone who has had the shock of monitoring their alcohol intake with an app will immediately know what I'm talking about. And doctors will tell you that reformed smokers always claim the level of their daily habit was higher than they admitted at the time they were actually smoking. To get the most accurate information possible, the way the questions are asked in the survey makes a very big difference. Asking what a customer did yesterday, or the last time they had occasion to use the product, gives a more accurate reading than asking them to generalize – that's when wishful thinking or faulty recollection kicks in. A person would be more likely to admit to drinking a whole bottle of wine yesterday than drinking a bottle a day in general. As long as enough customers are interviewed across a typical consumption interval for the category of product, the aggregated data is accurate because you will capture the broad spread of behaviour. For example, you will also be interviewing the folk who did not drink anything yesterday as well as those who did, giving an accurate overall picture.

The global market research market was worth $73.4 billion in 2019 according to Statista, doubling since 2008 and growing by 4% per annum. Companies that conduct this research in consumer markets include Nielsen, Kantar, Ipsos GfK and IRI. Other, more specialist market research companies in the global top ten include IQVIA (healthcare), Westat (US health, economics and transport), Wood Mackenzie (energy, mining, chemicals), INTAGE Group (consumer panel and retail in Japan and Asia). Whatever you want to measure, there is probably a company that is measuring it.

And this approach is not beyond the capability of smaller businesses. For our fictitious Seatown pizzeria, we might interview

The risk with asking customers themselves what they do is that claimed behaviour is often quite different from actual behaviour.

people out and about in the town or on the beach and discover that our customers are: families who take a break in Seatown, typically for one week, who go to restaurants for dinner three times while they are there, with a special meal on the last night of the holiday, which is normally Saturday. We might also have found out that they spend on average £100 ($130) for the weekday meals and £150 ($200) on the last night. This could help us deliver a special product (meal package) – the Saturday Splash!

Behaviour: watching and learning

Of course, brands can and do dig even deeper into the behaviour of their customers and, with such a wealth of digital data available, can uncover many new insights, or validate hypotheses because the correlations are now possible to check. There are specialist companies that do exactly this and they use many techniques to uncover new insights into customer behaviour, including 'listening' to 'conversations' on social media. One company I know was asked to uncover new food trends for one of the biggest global food and drink manufacturers. They collected social media posts from locations known to be the sites of street food markets and analyzed customer posts to identify which new things were becoming popular.

That the arrival of digital has transformed the availability of data about who customers are and what they do is not in doubt. The challenge is often that there is so much data that organizations struggle to make sense of it. One major international telecoms provider had to bring in a global consultancy firm to help them sort this out – that tells you the scale of the potential mess and the extent of the desperation!

Data is, of course, wonderful, but until recently, you could interrogate it but you had to know what to ask or what to look for. But now artificial intelligence (AI) allows organizations to find things that they weren't looking for. Finding an emergent behaviour that no one has yet noticed will give competitive advantage. At present AI is more commonly used to personalize marketing or to provide real-time alerts if consumers' behaviour is not as predicted, but its potential as a tool to unlock the deep understanding of customer behaviour is thrilling. Even more significant is its use for the understanding of disease, with brands such as the Roche, GlaxoSmithKline and AstraZeneca, not to mention countries' state health systems, all being the beneficiaries of these customer insights.

From the first twinkle to the sale
There are many brands whose focus is digital and whose founders are digital natives, the latter priding themselves on creating brands that were 'born digital'. However, most involve at a minimum the delivery of a product that has been ordered online. And customer behaviour needs to be tracked in both the online and the offline world, involving the intersection of an organization's own data and more conventional forms of market research.

Finding an emergent behaviour that no one has yet noticed will give competitive advantage.

Online-only brands can concentrate largely on the data they hold. B2B software providers (at least those that don't have a sales force, consultancy service or call centre) and online gaming are prime examples. But companies in this category should also know what prompts a person to download their package or app or to use it on any given day – and that is where your own data, however magnificent, will have its limitations.

I think there is no substitute for mapping your 'customer journey' to fully understand what your customer does, from end to end – from the first twinkle in their eye suggesting they have a need that you might fulfil to transacting with you (in the broadest sense of what that might involve) and, beyond that, to recommending you. Many of the insights gleaned will be marketing challenges; some will tell you the opportunities for your brand.

This chapter has covered the foundations of customer understanding which are indispensable for defining and building your brand: who your customers are, what they do and, importantly, how many of them there are. But you also need to know what makes people tick, so you can better create something that they will desire and select in preference to others and that they can love and be loyal to. That's what we look at in the next chapter.

CHAPTER 5

What makes your customers tick?

Knowing who your customers are, what they do and how many of them there are forms the foundations of customer understanding. But to create an even more desirable brand you should build on this and figure out what is on their minds and in their hearts.

Standard quantitative surveys look at attitudes, and these can be very helpful, especially if you don't have the budget to commission your own large-scale survey. Then there is 'qualitative research', where you take a smaller number of representative customers and interview them in depth. Often the qualitative research exploring attitudes and deeper feelings is conducted first. Then, once insights are unearthed, quantitative research is conducted to establish how widespread a particular attitude or feeling is, or to test alternatives where several have been uncovered. The fairly well-known 'focus group' is just one popular form of qualitative research, and 'depth interviews', where the people are interviewed one on one, are another.

I have also found, in organizations where research budgets are tiny, that a good chat with those who face the customers daily will tell you much about customers' motivations. For example, in a B2B enterprise, a chat with the sales team and a good look at how they hone their pitches to customers is a good way to better customer understanding.

And lastly, looking beyond market research can unearth particularly rich insights: for example, I have found them in academic papers and by speaking to psychologists. These are

> **In organizations where research budgets are tiny, a good chat with those who face the customers daily will tell you much about customers' motivations.**

often very revealing access points to a large sample of customers.

Customers will rarely tell you their deepest motivations directly. Unlike asking them if they drove to work yesterday, or whether they drank wine or cleaned their loo (it can be quite a day for customers sometimes!), they are pretty unlikely to be able to deconstruct why they do what they do or even to admit to more embarrassing behaviour. They won't tell you that they often eat chocolate to stop them yelling at their kids, that they feel inadequate when looking at magazines or that they can no longer function without their smartphones. All these insights are true and ones I have used to build brands. To get to these deeper human motivations, you need to find subtle ways for customers to reveal themselves.

Qualitative research: the focus group

The most common form of qualitative research is the 'focus group' – a term invented by Ernest Dichter, an American psychologist and market researcher. 'Group discussions', as they were known when I began my career, have been around since the 1940s, when Columbia University used them to research radio soap operas. Essentially what each focus group involves is a structured discussion, led by a trained researcher, with a group of about eight individuals who are the kind of people you are targeting with your brand. To ensure that the findings represent general customer opinion, you would seek to conduct at least four of these groups.

The composition of the groups is carefully considered and will very much depend on what you are seeking to find out. The demographic composition will almost always be considered, as might the level of usage of the category, product or brand. And then the likelihood of those individuals being comfortable with each other will be a factor – it is rare to mix genders because this is generally believed to minimize honesty, since men and women can try to impress each other! If you were researching people who were regular players of online games, you would not mix teenage boys with older women (Fortnite and Candy Crush!). The exception to this is the so called 'conflict group', where customers who have strong opposing views about a brand or category or are loyalists of competing brands are mixed together. The argument that generally ensues is a rich source of insight into the passions of the two tribes. Companies typically end up conducting six to eight focus groups, with at least two per customer cluster.

Focus groups used always to be conducted in someone's home or in a research facility, the latter having a two-way mirror so the brand owner or their agency could observe their customers. Nowadays virtual groups are very common, with the virtual world taking the place of the face-to-face gatherings. Alternatively, asynchronous research can be done, where the respondents interact with each other over several days by means of an online bulletin board.

The person that conducts the discussion (the moderator) is a trained, accredited researcher and lets the people there (the respondents) know that they are accredited and independent of the company that has commissioned the research. This evokes more frankness from the respondents. The sessions usually last around two hours and often involve getting responses to stimuli such as written statements, pictures or film clips. In addition, the respondents can be asked to sort pictures to bring to life how they feel about different brands. The discussion should be pretty free-flowing; each person is encouraged to have their say and emerging thoughts and feelings are drawn out. Moderating these groups requires outstanding listening skills and ability to manage the input from all participants.

Getting under the skin of people and getting to the bottom of their innermost thoughts is a real art. A qualitative researcher I know feels that a more unstructured decision is more revealing. He calls these 'un-focus groups'. One example he told me about was research he did into laundry detergent for a major global

A moderator directs a focus group while clients watch through a one-way mirror.

manufacturer. He asked women just to chat among themselves about how they felt when they did the laundry. Before long it became pretty obvious how they felt, which was summed up as: 'Sometimes I hate my children when I do their laundry.' How the manufacturer dealt with this insight I don't know, but one way it could be leveraged might be to position the brand as a 'superhero', showing that doing laundry is a challenge, as opposed to the more commonly adopted position portraying it as an act of care for the family.

Many companies are unsettled by negative insights like this, but they have never worried me, as long as you don't make it obvious to the customer what you know about them. The customer needs their problems solved and that is the job the brand should just get on and do. I don't think it's the brand owner's job to like or not like the customer's need.

Qualitative research: even greater depths

Sometimes it is better to interview your customer one-to-one. To ensure you have a sufficient sample of customers, you need to talk to about two dozen people, but one-to-one research is much more time-consuming for the researcher and therefore more expensive. It tends therefore to be chosen only when absolutely necessary. Typically, this is the case if the matter under investigation is very sensitive, such as health-related issues. Or if the presence of others would undermine honesty because of loss of face or the existence of 'bragging rights'. Examples that spring to mind are condoms, dating apps, or more mundane areas such as shaving for men. Sometimes the customer would not agree to attend a focus group, such as senior corporate executives, who are not only busy but would have confidentiality concerns if gathered with a group of their peers. Depth interviews can be conducted face to face, but they often happen via video conference or simply on the telephone. The same techniques as in focus groups will get individuals to open up, although what is missing is the stimulation drawn from the presence of other customers.

Ethnography is another type of research and is my favourite, because it involves observing customers like an anthropologist and chatting to them in situ, rather than asking questions. I like it because the customer is in their natural habitat, so what is observed is likely to be more truthful and revealing. It is a methodology that requires a great deal of skill in those who conduct it, and it is costly. When we embarked on a brand revamp for one of Mondelez's most valuable chocolate brands, Milka, we felt this was a good methodology to choose because people are often a bit disingenuous about their consumption of chocolate, especially adults, who generally say it's for the children and fib about how much of it they eat themselves!

In this case, we recruited families from Russia, Serbia, France, Germany and Poland to take part in the study. It was a 'deprivation study' – an established industry methodology, as the name suggests, where you ask the participants not to consume the category of product in question and see what this and their return to consumption reveals. We observed, gently interrogated and filmed families in their homes when their milk chocolate was restored after three weeks without. We discovered that chocolate was found to be a soothing antidote to the stresses and strains of everyday life. People often had a few squares on arrival home from work to calm them down and to engage with their families in a better mood. Despite looking forward to being with their loved ones all day, they were disappointed in how grumpy they often were by the time they got home.

Milka's creamy texture is especially soothing and all chocolate contains the mood enhancer, theobromine, so we connected our insight that our customers needed to be soothed with our product, one that is particularly good at evoking nicer, kinder feelings. We summarised this as Milka awakens your sweet nature. Milk chocolate makes you nicer. Who knew?

> **We discovered that chocolate was a soothing antidote to the stresses and strains of everyday life.**

A different way in

Using unconventional means of getting to the bottom of customers' true feelings is another favourite of mine. When we developed Dove's 'Campaign for Real Beauty', we started with a hypothesis that beauty ads made women feel bad about themselves, based on the reaction of the (mostly female) team to a selection of ads. To be sure that this was a widespread feeling, we consulted psychologists specializing in female self-image and self-esteem, notably Susie Orbach (author of *Fat Is a Feminist Issue*, who, famously, treated Princess Diana for bulimia), and Catherine Steiner-Adair, a Harvard professor specializing in eating disorders. They were vehement in their validation of our hypothesis and pointed us in the direction of numerous academic studies that proved it. One study showed that girls' self-esteem dropped by ten points after reading a beauty magazine. The impact of the introduction of commercial TV to Fiji coincided with the development of bulimia, which had previously been nonexistent. How this insight transformed the brand is referred to throughout the book.

Quantitative research on thoughts and feelings

If you are a wealthy enough brand, you can validate and attach numbers to qualitative insights with quantitative research. Typically, you will commission a survey and ask for levels of agreement with a simple statement or ask questions about a statement or a picture (or both) that brings the insight to life. Or you could test different ways to express the insight and see how people respond at scale. Qualitative research is good enough on its own to unearth a true insight, but it won't tell you how many people feel like that. Nor will it give you more detail about which demographics are more or less likely to feel that way or which behaviours correlate most strongly to those feelings. All this stuff is useful to know but critical when building a marketing plan where the channels of media and distribution will be analyzed by demography and some general aspects of behaviour. Sometimes, even more importantly, boards and finance directors often insist on knowing numbers before investing millions in a new brand, product or ad campaign that depends on that insight. And who can blame them?

Boards and finance directors often insist on knowing numbers before investing millions in a new brand. And who can blame them?

Psychographic segmentation

Psychographic segmentation is a posh name for grouping customers by attitudes or beliefs, and it is often obtained from general surveys instead of the more bespoke approach outlined above. There are many surveys conducted globally which have measured attitudes across whole populations for decades. For example, Kantar's TGI survey asks a battery of very general questions about what people think and feel, in which people are invited to agree or disagree with such statements as 'I believe it is worth paying more for good quality' or 'I like to stand out in a crowd' or 'Computers confuse me, I'll never get used to them.'

Customers who claim to buy certain popular brands are also tracked by the survey, so you can find out which attitudes are highly prevalent in purchasers of any of these brands. From this data, you will be able to find out what users of your brand and its competitors tend to think or believe and whether there are any interesting differences. Or if your brand is not big enough to be tracked, you can use the most similar one as a proxy.

And, because this is quantitative data, you can also tell your board and CFO (chief financial officer) how many of any particular type of customers there are. Even more excitingly, you can look further to see which other groups in the population are more or less likely to hold those attitudes and you may be able to identify potential customers where you might not have looked before.

For example, let's say you are an energy drink. You may have assumed your customers engage regularly in sport, are upmarket and are much more likely to be male. But when you looked at this data, you found your brand indexed very highly with the attitude statement 'I like to go out and get drunk' (yes, they really do ask that). And further digging reveals that this attitude is held most strongly by young downmarket customers, with no gender bias. Further investigation shows that some individuals are already using your drink as a hangover cure. There are also more people in this segment than the one in which you operate now. You could tut your disapproval, but most commercially minded businesses would seriously explore the potential. You could then create new products in your range to appeal to downmarket young drinkers of all genders and make an even more performance-enhancing variant to reinforce the brand for your sporty upmarket males. Ten years later, updates to this same data reveal that Generation Z are highly likely to be teetotal, but very much into mindfulness and mental well-being… and so a new generation of needs is born for a new generation of customers. And the bright, customer-centric brand can fulfil these emerging needs. This is a fictional example, but the evolution of the Lucozade product range in the UK (page 26) might suggest it was a true story.

Of course, smaller, bespoke surveys can also get to the bottom of what your potential customers think and feel. Then use desk research or educated guesswork to give you a good estimate of the number of people having those same feelings in the population and therefore the business opportunity for your brand.

Using the segmentation

Sophisticated organizations will sanity-check the potential segmentations to make sure that a segment is big enough to make it worth targeting, and see whether it is growing or not and whether there is a lot of competition for those customers. A second-best segment might be a better option if it is bigger, faster-growing and not the focus of much competitive effort. Another aspect could be that one group of customers might be very price-sensitive and therefore less profitable. At Vodafone, we chose not to target our 'technologically literate' segment because they were savvy on deals and were the least profitable segment of the seven customer segments we identified. Actually, this was a surprise – we would have thought that their enthusiasm for technology would have made them willing to pay more. But it was the customers whose attitude to technology was more mainstream that were more profitable.

Many bigger firms recruit a bespoke panel of customers who agree to be surveyed on a regular basis about almost anything, and this is so much easier to do in the digital age. You used to have to phone them up! They can be a representative sample of the whole population, but if you have defined your customer segments, it makes sense to recruit customers who fit the profile, either of your target segments or including those you are not focused on. We had such a panel at Vodafone and it was useful not only to identify the big longer-term needs (video streaming on mobiles at home, for instance) but also to ask very 'quick and dirty' questions – for instance, we wanted to know how many of our customers had watched the TV show *Breaking Bad*, which we planned to feature in a new ad campaign.

Many bigger firms recruit a bespoke panel of customers who agree to be surveyed on a regular basis about almost anything, and this is so much easier to do in the digital age.

Painting a picture of your customer

Bringing all this together and combining all the information you can glean from demographics, behaviour, qualitative research and psychographics enables you to paint a picture of the customer which brings them to life in the organization.

It may be that the customer is defined by one major thing, but often more interesting and differentiating definitions come from combinations. And, however you have arrived at a succinct definition, to make the understanding of the customer clear and concise, it helps to give your customer a label or a name. This helps in larger organizations to both chat about the customer easily and to drive speedy understanding. For example:

Premium fashion brand: Attention-seeking sensorialists.

Sports drink: Performance enhancers. Big night outers. Mindful millennials.

Logistics firm: Diligent sceptics.

An example I recall at Vodafone was a segment called 'Family Connectors'. These were people who wanted to be at the centre of everything but struggled to do all the things they'd like. The role of mobile in their lives was to connect their family circle; they loved apps with a purpose and wanted to balance their busy lives. They were ABC1 25–55 with a male bias and tended to live in the south of the UK. Just saying 'Family Connectors' evokes a picture of who your brand is for and makes it easy for anyone in the organization to remember it and then to think of the best way to serve them.

Another theoretical example could be for our 'Diligent Sceptics' in procurement in the global B2B market. We might flesh this out as follows: 'Diligent Sceptics' have been around the block of corporate procurement too many times to take at face value the claims of any salesman. They know their job depends on getting things 100 per cent right, so they make no apology for demanding a lot of information and like to test the services before buying anything. Typically, middle class and male aged between 35 and 55, they are often found in corporate tax havens such as Liechtenstein or Switzerland and cities where big global HQs are typically sited, especially Chicago, New York, Frankfurt, London, Shanghai and Singapore.

For the Seatown pizzeria: 'Harmony-seeking holidaying parents.' They know that if the kids are happy then they are happy. And they are even happier if the kids are consuming anything other than junk food or junk drinks. They are slightly upmarket and tend to live in cities in the same country or state as Seatown. The Seatown trip will be their second holiday; the main family holiday is further afield, possibly abroad.

There is a peculiar tendency to do so-called 'pen portraits' of customers, where they are given a fictitious name. I find this plain daft. If you take our Vodafone example, it becomes something like 'Ben, 40, wants to be at the centre of everything but struggles to … etc etc'. I dislike this approach because it is reductive: our customer is not exclusively male (and this suggests he is) and is not 40 but between a range of ages. Even more ridiculously, the name becomes a shorthand in internal discussions for the customer segment, with conversations about whether we are targeting 'Bens' or 'Tyrones'. To anyone other than the brand team, this random taxonomy is impenetrable gobbledegook. Given its lack of utility it is a bafflingly common practice; my thesis is that it gives organizations the illusion of customer understanding and intimacy, which might compensate for the fact that it is actually lacking. Give me real understanding and genuine intimacy any day.

Pulling it all together

Once all the information is gathered, a core summary featuring the most important insight needs to be written to define the brand. The framework I find the most useful captures all the key themes and covers who the customer is and what they do, think and want. This is then expressed relative to their lives, the category and the brand. In so doing, you will find a 'sweet spot' where the insight is relevant not only to their consumption of your brand but also to their lives. This enables the brand to be more pertinent and PR-friendly, as Chapter 8 explains. Two examples are illustrated to make this clear.

Once all the information is gathered, a core summary featuring the most important insight needs to be written to define the brand.

Understanding customers takes a lot of work. But it is the biggest single thing that companies can do to create powerful, enduring brands and outstandingly effective marketing. Amazon, now the biggest company in the world, describes itself as customer-obsessed. I rest my case.

Consumer map example 1: milk chocolate

What do consumers	Life	Category	Brand
Do	Struggle to balance the demands of work and family life	Reach for chocolate when my nerves need soothing	Savour the sweet and melting texture
Think/ Believe/ Feel	The demands of life make me difficult to be with sometimes	A hit of chocolate will shift my mood when I need it	Soothes me better than other chocolates
Want	Harmony to abound with the people I love	To be my best self with the ones I love	To melt away the cares of my day

Consumer map example 2: digital recruitment platform for senior executives

What do consumers	Life	Category	Brand
Do	Push the boundaries just a little at work, but within the confines of what is acceptable demands of work and family life	Use the bigger search firms to hire, occasionally leavening the pack with a firm that is a bit more interesting	Have heard the name of brand X in the context of search
Think/ Believe/ Feel	Making an impact involves some risk.	It ain't exactly broke, but I still have an itch to fix it	It's a new thingummy. Uberish.
Want	Risks to pay off, magnificently!	Talent choices that delight and for which I will be appreciated	Nothing much/at best find out more

CHAPTER 6

What makes your brand different?

Coco Chanel got it in one: 'To be irreplaceable, one must always be different.' Her quote is my top pick on the benefits of differentiation. Every brand manager or CEO I have ever met aspires to have the customer want their product or service to the exclusion of all others. Yet, in almost every instance, they adopt category norms and follow their competition in product innovation and marketing activities. On what basis is the customer expected to make a choice if there's not much difference between the offerings? And then those CEOs wonder why they are in a price-sensitive market! The only way to make brand owners wake up, in my experience, is to confront them with all their competitors' products, websites, advertisements and activities alongside their own on a wall. I mean, literally, pinned up on a wall, right in front of them. It is a salutary and humbling experience, so worth it on two counts.

> '**To be irreplaceable, one must always be different.**'
>
> Coco Chanel

Brands don't have to do every single thing differently from their competitors to stand out. There are some things that the customer absolutely will not compromise on, known as the hygiene factors. But brands need to consider every aspect that they could reasonably choose to vary and decide what to do differently. And what not to do. A full day figuring this out is a very good use of a senior executive's time.

What follows are some of the things that brands should look at to assess how they stack up versus the competition, but that list can vary – you need to choose the aspects that matter most in your category. Doing this may also unearth underleveraged but distinctive brand assets. And you should pay as much attention to the 'how' as to the 'what' of brands.

Themes and conclusions should be drawn from the whole review to find an overarching point of differentiation that can guide the development of many aspects of the brand and its marketing. There will also be opportunities for differentiation that are worth acting on in each matter under review, but which won't necessarily contribute to the big brand differentiator.

What your organization offers

This is dealt with in more depth in the next chapter but, clearly, having a product that does something truly different is the holy grail. In the 19th and early 20th centuries this was much more likely than it is now. As the consumer era emerged so did the idea of the 'unique selling proposition', or USP, a term that emerged in the 1940s from advertising agency Ted Bates. In some categories, the USP does still exist, especially in the early days of a category's emergence. But the truth is, a *unique* selling proposition is a rare beast. Continual striving to do something better than others for your customer is the very essence of brand building and marketing. The problem with USPs is that they are rarely unique for long, as nowadays competitors can copy you very quickly, especially in the digital space. As this is a practical guide and this is a chapter on differentiation, I'll acknowledge this and simply say that of course brands should review what products their competitors offer. They should do this if only to neutralize the delusion that what they offer is genuinely unique, and when the light dawns, find another, more sustainable, way to be different. The exercise can also help identify who the closest competitors are and a group one might choose to watch more closely.

Brand names and logos

Changing a brand name and logo is a pretty radical step and, if the company has been around a while, not a decision that should be taken lightly. If your name and logo are long-established, I would not risk wholesale change for the sake of being different, but might evolve it a bit if it's very similar to everyone else's. If customers select your brand spontaneously and quickly, how recognizable it is matters a lot, and logos, colours and shape are good places to start. If you are launching a brand, do the review of competitors before naming it and starting to design your logo.

A brand positioning project I did for a diversity consultancy was an object lesson in undifferentiated logo design. Almost all the logos of the competitors were either purple or rainbow/multicoloured. One can see how each company got to that point. 'We can't align with either gender, so we can't be pink or blue, so let's go for purple!' Or, 'Let's represent our business with multicolours, as this represents inclusivity and diversity.' Very laudable and logical, but such thinking done in isolation created no distinctiveness … and, other colours are available!

In the UK, there are three mobile network operators competing with Vodafone: O_2, EE and Three. When I was UK Director of Brand Marketing at Vodafone UK, I did this competitive exercise and discovered that its name was an under-leveraged brand asset, and this thinking contributed to the positioning for the company. Vodafone was the only company to have the same name it started with (in the 1980s). Most of the other brands were new and created by mergers or demergers; EE resulted from the T-Mobile and Orange merger, O_2 emerged when Telefonica bought the network from British Telecom, and Three was a brand created for the 3G spectrum launch by Hutchison Whampoa, which used to own Orange! If you want to make your head spin while simultaneously losing the will to live, look at the history of mobile brands in the UK. And your marketer's heart will sink when you see beautifully built brands exterminated with apparently little remorse, most notably Orange.

Vodafone, however, was an organization that had stood the test of time. Vodafone as a name stands out from EE, Three and O_2, and these were undoubtedly less true to their roots, having been relatively newly minted and invented by marketers. Considering other aspects of our culture and ethics and our competitors' tendency towards lightheartedness, we combined all this into a summation of our difference: 'Vodafone is a brand of substance in a sea of superficiality.'

If customers select your brand spontaneously and quickly, how recognizable it is matters a lot.

Slogans and positioning

Slogans – what is on Google's title tags, on the landing pages of a website or in 'About us' sections – help to get to the bottom of what your competitors stand for or offer. If you are planning to have a slogan, you need to ensure it is different from those of your competitors. You would hope a brand's slogan would give a clue to its positioning (and some do), but the vast majority don't.

Nowhere is this truer than in B2B. Some years ago, I was creating a brand strategy for a small custom software development firm where I was the interim marketing director. Of course, I looked at slogans as part of the work on differentiation. They were a pretty much a random assemblage of the same four or five words.

Here are examples of 10 of the 16 competitors I reviewed at the time. Note the repetition of 'performance', 'delivering' and 'solutions':

Advanced Software Limited: Delivering business improvement.
Micar: Building software solutions.
Pinesoft: Partners for Performance.
RSK: Bug solutions.
Decoded Solutions: Delivering Truly Bespoke
  Business solutions.
Sopra Steria: Delivering Transformation together.
Accenture: High Performance Delivered.
And **CGI Inc** invited us at that time to 'Experience the
  Commitment'. No idea!

Just two stood out and were thankfully free of random capitalizations:

Dev Team SSN: Your idea made real.
Box UK: Simply brilliant thinkers making software
  brilliantly simple.

What we did learn was that getting a great and clear slogan would help to differentiate us and that anything featuring 'solutions', 'performance' and 'delivery' would be a no-no.

If the slogan doesn't give you the clue to what the brand is all about, you need to look a little further into their communication, search and websites being my usual first port of call.

In B2B there is a sector that should know how to do positioning well – advertising agencies. When at Mondelez I was a global advertiser looking for a global agency for one of our brands and Googled some candidates to see if they might be suitable. It was not an edifying experience then and, sadly, it isn't now. I replicated the task on the day of writing this, and below is what I found in the title tags in a Google search for some of the biggest agencies in the world. This is the first thing a customer sees, and it is messaging the companies can control.

The only truly differentiated proposition here belongs to Saatchi & Saatchi, with second prize going to Grey. Several of the offerings are worse than undifferentiated. They are often a privileged glimpse of the obvious, in my opinion, featuring incomplete sentences cut off by the character limit.

If you want to be differentiated as a global advertising agency, a positioning based on 'global', 'worldwide', 'advertising' or 'brands' is not going to make you stand out. I am beyond disappointed in a sector that ought to know better.

BBDO Worldwide:
'Advertising agency BBDO Worldwide's homepage, where you can explore recent work, news, knowledge and see a summary of their history…'

Saatchi & Saatchi:
The Lovemarks company. Nothing is impossible.

Grey Advertising Global:
Famously Effective since 1917.

Wunderman Thompson:
We exist to inspire growth for ambitious brands. We are part creative agency, part consultancy and part technology company.

McCann Worldgroup:
Global network of advertising agencies.

Ogilvy:
We design the brand; we turn the brand into an experience and we communicate the brand's story.

Publicis Groupe:
Founded in 1926, we are the world's third largest communications group known for its world-renowned creativity, best in class technology and…..

DDB:
Highly ranked, worldwide advertising agency.

Leo Burnett:
Leo Burnett worldwide is a globally active agency based in Chicago. Learn more about career opportunities, our work, culture and…..

McCann Worldgroup:
Global network of advertising agencies.

Wieden + Kennedy:
Here's where we post our latest and greatest work from all our offices.

Dentsu Inc:
The Dentsu Website includes corporate information, information about our business, press releases, investor relations information, CSR…..

People and culture

Customers will often experience a brand through its employees, whether through retail colleagues, call centres or salespeople. If this is the case, company culture can be a major source of differentiation and worth trying to figure out for your competitors.

Lush, a cosmetics retailer with strongly ethical credentials and trading in 49 countries worldwide, delivers as much of its point of difference by the way customers are treated in store as with its products. The beauty category adopts pretty hard-sell tactics in general – anyone who has experienced the perfume snipers in a department store or been the victim of the Orogold hawkers in any one of 15 countries will know exactly what I mean. Lush declares publicly that its customer experience is what sets it apart and describes its staff as enthusiastic, knowledgeable and passionate. Both the recruitment policies and practice encourage inclusivity, individualism and an expressive and personable character. Retail staff are trained to take pride in selling people only what they need and only what's right for them. Lush links this to its ethical credentials, in that selling a customer the wrong product results in waste and pollution. It is not a surprise to me that this approximately $1 billion turnover brand grew 46-fold between 2000 (£17.6 million) and 2019 (£977 million) – the last normal year of trading before the coronavirus pandemic.

Furthermore, Lush pays its retail staff more than competitors and was the first chain store to adopt the higher 'Living Wage' in 2011 for store colleagues. If the staff of a company deliver significant brand differentiation, why would you not invest in that?

If the staff of a company deliver significant brand differentiation, why would you not invest in that?

Visual equities

Do you look different from your competition? What colour are your competitors? If access through an app is a key gateway to your brand, does your app pop on a smartphone? Do you have a mascot or an icon? So many aspects of visual identity can be reviewed: you just need to pick the four or five that are most relevant to you. Look at ads if that's where your competition show up; look at storefronts if in retail; if you're in a B2B market with high web traffic, review websites; if apps are the name of your game… you get the picture! What follows are some examples of aspects to review rather than an exhaustive list.

Does your product look different from your competition,

and what distinguishes it? The Land Rover Defender is uber-chunky and boxy and I would imagine that its brand differentiation could be something like 'uncompromising ruggedness'. For other automotive products, their look might not dictate the overarching point of difference for the whole brand but might be a differentiating aspect worth preserving, like BMW's double front grille.

Colour is another aspect to consider. When I did this review for Vodafone, their brand colour was red, and all the UK competitors were blueish. This was a delightful discovery for me. There was much discussion at the time about minimizing the redness of our physical estate, for no good reason apparent to me. We were in the midst of a redesign of the Customer Experience Centre (CEC) for our corporate clients (who accounted for a very large percentage of our turnover), which was being refurbished under my guidance. Of course, lots of bright red as an interior colour would not be a restful environment, but the first designs for the CEC that I saw were 100 per cent monochromatic. Very serious, very corporate, but did not build our brand in the least. So I reintroduced dashes of red in the CEC, and when we came to refit the retail estate about 12 months later and I had celebrated our redness in our brand strategy, we had fallen back in love with red. Furthermore, it had become a strategic discussion, not a schoolyard-calibre spat among executives about favourite colours. You'd be surprised how often nonsense like this goes on in many companies; the biggest bully gets to pick the colour – unless there's a strategy!

Reviewing the app icons your competitors use on the mobile interface is relevant if customers switch between providers. This matters more if you are an airline or a computer game than

Airline app icons on a tablet screen. EasyJet's orange creates standout.

if you are a bank, for example, as the typical customer will most likely use only one bank but many games and several airlines. When you choose who to fly with for your next holiday, you won't miss the bright orange easyJet logo on your phone.

The other sense in which icons exist is in the characters that brands use, the Milka cow for instance, or the Pillsbury Doughboy. Customers loved the lilac Milka cow, and we chose to make more of her as the star in our TV commercials. Most icons are particular to the brand, but some categories do have similar icons. For example, pouring milk pops up on many milk chocolate packs and, at Cadbury, we changed the graphics to more closely link the 'glass and a half' claim with the Cadbury logo.

Packaging

If your product will be picked off a shelf in a matter of seconds by your customer, your packaging had better be different from the brands that sit all around it. The challenge with this is the retailer own brands, which often copy the brand leader and erode its distinctiveness. Just look at the purple milk chocolate bars sitting near Cadbury Dairy Milk and the lilac ones near Milka. A great example of the use of packaging to establish distinctiveness is Clipper Tea (Cupper in Germany), with matt packaging and attractive and quirkily crafted graphics. This differentiation, I believe, is as much a driver of their success as their ethical and sustainable credentials. It's also a way that smaller brands can punch above their weight, as having stylish pack graphics doesn't cost a lot more than packaging without it. Pack shape can also be significantly differentiating, but changing it can be costly – tens of millions to retool factories for a large grocery brand.

Having stylish pack graphics doesn't cost a lot more than packaging without it.

Communication

This covers everything from your website to your advertising to emails – however you connect with customers. And you should assess both the look of them and their tone of voice.

A great example of this is in the women's beauty haircare category, where what I like to call 'Olympic hair' is ubiquitous. Great-looking hair is a benefit that customers want to see writ large, so one would vary this at one's peril. As a result, how the ads look is not a source of much differentiation in the category.

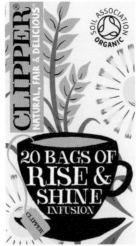

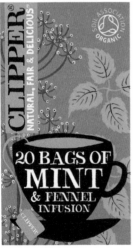

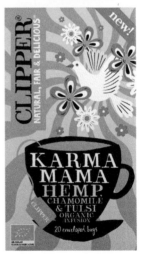

Clipper tea packaging.

But I take my hat off to the brand Aussie, which selected black and white photography…and the women clearly have amazing hair. This makes Aussie stand out visually and suggests a rejection of the gloss and fakery of the category. It also differentiates on tone of voice, with a down-to-earth cheekiness that is most definitely lacking from the other leading beauty haircare brands. L'Oréal Elvive, Garnier, Pantene and TRESemmé are in glorious technicolour and take themselves much more seriously. Aussie might have distilled all this and defined its difference as 'down-to-earth', which is consistent with Australian heritage. And you see that expressed in other aspects of the brand, such as its packaging, which is not as blingy as its competitors.

Once you've drawn conclusions from what your competitors are doing, you can settle on something that will make you stand out.

At Mondelez, when we were figuring out Milka, we identified that many chocolate ads in the category showed self-indulgent moments. Knowing that we were targeting families and that connectedness was a big desire for our customers, the brand team decided that Milka would be a 'we brand' not a 'me brand' as its primary differentiation. Over time, this impacted not only our advertising campaigns but also product development, with, for example, bagged, bite-sized chocolates designed for sharing.

In B2B, it's normally the website that is the shop window. Working with an executive search firm recently, I discovered that the category norm for websites was to showcase 'impossibly attractive executives working in impossibly shiny buildings'. The firm I was advising had a strong customer base in chief technology officers and chief financial officers. Its innovative tech-enabled platform had three core benefits that delivered a multiplier effect. We decided to use abstract images representing exponentials, including tree branches and Fibonacci gears. I always suspected that the company felt uncomfortable with looking so different, despite believing it was a disruptor in its category. But I guess that is the existential crisis of being different and, therefore, irreplaceable.

User imagery is often used in communication because people are influenced by who else they perceive to be using the product. Commonly used marketing tactics include: celebrities or a particular type of model in ads; rewards for a particular vlogger recommending the product; stories in a newspaper or magazine where a celebrity just happens to be 'papped' carrying the brand, which, of course, they were given; or someone who uses it in

Examples of user imagery evoking differing characteristics.

wholesome

adventurous

urbane

their show on TV. One thing that's pretty certain is that such instances do not generally happen by accident, so they signal something about the positioning of your competitors.

Once you've drawn conclusions from what your competitors are doing, you can settle on something that will make you stand out. If they are all squeaky clean in terms of user imagery, you might go a bit grungy or rebellious. You don't have to use grungy celebrities or rebels in your marketing, but the concept can help you define your difference. When you've figured out all that, it's time to resurrect this analysis and decide whether to adopt user imagery as a part of your marketing strategy.

Routes to market

Where your product is sold and the online company it keeps can make a difference to how your brand is perceived and can also be a legitimate source of differentiation. For instance, if you were a premium healthy food brand, the discovery that all your competition was stocked in Whole Foods but not at a high-end retailer such as Waitrose or Trader Joe's might lead you to choose to focus your brand on quality rather than organic credentials.

Digital distribution in all its forms is eroding distribution as a means of understanding and delivering differentiation. Forces such as programmatic media buying (where algorithms pick where your ad appears), aggregator sites and the simple ubiquity of Amazon's offer are used more and more by all brands. And these channels and techniques are here to stay because of their genius at building businesses. But they don't tell you much about differentiation because all brands are in the same places. So, if you and your competition all rely on identical channels of digital distribution, you won't find out much about your competitors from this aspect of their marketing.

Don't forget to be relevant

It is vital that your differentiation is relevant to your customers. At Vodafone, we had identified that customers were becoming more dependent practically and emotionally on their mobile phones as smartphones were increasingly adopted. A brand of substance was therefore very relevant to them. Who wants to lean on a joker?

I have come across one brand in my career where relevance and differentiation were locked in conflict, and that was Toblerone. Its triangular shape was much loved and its place in the gift market was strong, especially as a small present for men. You cannot miss it on any shelf. But it resisted all attempts to move it into the more everyday chocolate category, where its awkward shape and involving eat made it less relevant. And making it a different shape would have meant it was not really Toblerone at all!

As you do this review across a wide range of aspects, you will spot patterns and themes. Some analyses won't contribute to the overarching brand strategy but will be really useful to make your marketing distinctive. Overall, you should choose one big theme or pattern to guide your decisions for the whole brand. Something as simple as 'a brand of substance in a sea of superficiality', 'a "we" brand, not a "me" brand', or 'a down-to-earth brand in a hyperbolic, glossy category'. And you can also ensure that you retain those aspects you have identified as category hygiene factors. Not everything you do has to be different – just find what you need to do to help your customer choose you, prefer you and ultimately make you irreplaceable.

Not everything you do has to be different – just find what you need to do to help your customer choose you, prefer you and ultimately make you irreplaceable.

CHAPTER 7

What gives your brand the right to win?

The 'right to win' is my favoured term for what your brand does that fulfils what your customer wants or needs. Once upon a time, this part of a brand's strategy was known as the USP, the unique selling proposition. For example: 'New Glo washes whites whiter than any other detergent.' 'Washes whites whiter' is the USP.

The USP was arguably the most significant element of marketing thinking used since the 1940s, when it was invented by US advertising agency Ted Bates. Despite its age, some organizations continue to use it and the term is still common parlance in marketing. USPs tended to be based around functional performance, probably because they were invented when functional superiority and uniqueness were more achievable. And, in those times, the marketing didn't really need to go much further to sell the product. As markets became more crowded and USPs not so U, brands began to look at emotional, as well as functional, benefits to drive sales. These were less easy to prove but could be just as persuasive. For example: 'The whiteness of a shirt washed in New Glo makes you the most confident man in the boardroom.' (Well, we are talking last century, here!) The right to win would still be the whiteness of the wash in both of these examples.

Now that we live in a world of intense competition and the ability to copy almost anything at warp speed, uniqueness is very, very rare indeed and superior performance is short-lived. Also, the USP tends to lump product offering and differentiation into one. I think it is more useful to separate them. If you do, you have more opportunity to offer a relevant reason why your customers will want to buy your product but you can find other ways of being different, such as how you approach things, or your staff's attitude. It gives more flexibility and the opportunity to find a bigger, more relevant, more competitive and more sustainable overarching theme for your brand. Getting to this theme is explained further in Chapter 9.

If you have based your brand's raison d'être on functional performance, you will most likely find yourself engaged in a war of competitive claims. Worse still, performance improvements tend to happen in smaller and smaller increments over time. Often the end state is a margin of superior functionality that cannot even be discerned by the customer.

When you have identified what your brand's offer should be, there is a litmus test I recommend. Would you look a good friend in the eye and tell them they should buy that brand because of that reason? If you wouldn't, then don't have that as your right to win (or your USP, for that matter). And if you don't consider

The evolution of 'Washes Whiter' – Persil ads across the decades from the 1950s to the recent 'Dirt is good' campaign.

your customers to be your friends, you need to take a good hard look at yourself. They are paying your wages, after all.

Most marketing guides will tell you to make big, bold claims to get customers to choose your product or service. That is not the same thing as loudly trumpeting a minor margin of competitive superiority. And, as we will see, softer claims can be as big and as bold, and more appealing to customers. I often wonder if the tendency for performance-based branding is much more about the competitively oriented egos of the marketers than it is about the customer.

Would you look a good friend in the eye and tell them they should buy that brand because of that reason?

But hard or soft, big or small, bold or less so, you'd better be telling the truth when you make a claim about what your brand offers. Lying isn't popular with your god, the authorities or your customer.

A health warning about what you say

We live in an age where dissonance between claims and truth is called out very readily. A brand will simply not get away with claiming to be the biggest, fastest, greenest or whatever. In many countries, regulators can prevent organizations from making false claims in their communication or fine those that do, whether online or offline, or force them to change their claims. However, whatever the regime, if a brand does not do what it says it will, customers will bash it on review sites and trash it on social media. Arguably, the regulators are saving brands from themselves.

There is a pretty straightforward way to ensure your brand reputation is preserved: speak the truth about what your brand does. A well-expressed and positive version of the truth is fine, but it must be, at the core, the truth. Because advertising is such a public forum, its claims often damage brands and can cause their downfall. Some big companies that should know better have been severely punished for their transgressions, as we can see from the examples opposite.

The minute you put your head above the parapet and make a bold and definitive claim, a customer or a journalist will be after you to prove it false. So your new product development department had better be on it and have integrity. Or you'll be in the papers, in court, in jail, or – worse – all your customers will desert you and your company will fail. Or all four.

Collateral reputational damage and jail terms	In 2013, the food Safety Authority of Ireland found that horsemeat and pork were present in many products claiming to be 100% beef. There were very significant amounts of horse in one burger product. And as more products were tested a huge scandal erupted across Europe. Unravelling the supply chain was complicated and many interconnected companies were found to be knowingly and unknowingly involved. In one example meat originating from Romania was labelled clearly as horse and a company in France was found to be relabelling it as beef to enhance profits. Not only did the company responsible have its contracts cancelled but the directors were sentenced to jail six years later. New EU-wide legislation was enacted to improve supply-chain tracking and testing, but it was the brands the consumer knew and loved, the ones who withdrew the offending products as soon as they know about the tests (such as Aldi, Lidl, Tesco, Dunnes Stores, Iceland and Findus), that suffered collateral reputational damage.
$28 billion fine	Volkswagen was fined $28 billion as a criminal penalty in a Detroit court for putting software in its vehicles to allow them to pass diesel emissions tests in order to substantiate VW's 'clean diesel' claims.
$40 million fine	Skechers claimed their shoes helped to burn calories with each step – which is true, but so would any shoe, or no shoe at all. They settled claims costing them $40 million.
$20 million fine	Uber was forced by the USA's Federal Trade Commission to settle $20 million in claims that it had inflated hourly earnings for drivers in its online recruitment ads.
$9.5 million fine	Classmates.com was ordered by a US court to pay out a $9.5 million settlement to subscribers who were emailed to say old friends were trying to contact them and they could rekindle old friendships if they upgraded – which was untrue.

How to identify your best right to win?

I recommend selecting something that you do particularly well, that is relevant to your customer. If it is better or different from competition, so much the better, but it needn't be better than everyone else. Something that if nourished and communicated, you can keep up over time and that can inspire innovation. Even if it is the thing that you or your team just loves to do. It's a strategic thought, not a slogan, so clarity rather than poetry is key at this stage. The overall idea that could lead to your slogan will come later, when we figure out how to connect the dots between this and customer insight, cultural context and differentiation.

Here are some ways to think about finding 'your thing'.

What the product does or what the service offers

Despite the health warnings, this is a good place to start, but as you've probably gathered, I'd suggest not making it reliant on always being the very best at what you do!

Airbnb returned to their roots after the COVID crisis. Having recognized that they were perhaps diversifying too far and growing too quickly, and looking at the $1 billion wreckage wrought by the pandemic, the CEO and founder, Brian Chesky, has gone back to the company's values. At the time of writing, he is axing flight service, hotels, luxury homes and the customer magazine, deciding that they don't need to own the whole travel experience. He is reverting to what he describes as special about Airbnb: 'everyday people who host in their homes.' This is Airbnb's right to win, what made it great in the first place, and Chesky believes in its ability to drive future growth instead of the diversified path. One doesn't need a global pandemic to learn that lesson, but it is a valuable one. Diluting and becoming less special is not a path to success.

Meituan-Dianping is a Chinese super-app for more than 30 services related mostly to food, beverages and tourism, with user reviews, and integrated with payment and chat platforms. Its vision is to be the Amazon of services, and its history suggests that its right to win could be based on its ability to integrate and collaborate, whether with platforms or partnerships, both owned and external. This is a brilliant basis upon which to drive growth because it seems to have evolution embedded at its core, and the brand has grown from its inception in 2010 to an

Meituan-Dianping's integration and collaboration capability creates a lifestyle platform, delivering its aspiration to be the Amazon of services.

operating revenue of $13.7 billion in 2019, up 49.5 per cent from the previous year.

Here are some other famous examples born from the product's performance. The 'right to win' is assumed from their communication, as the strategy is not in the public domain.

DE BEERS:
Diamonds are
indestructible.
This became the famous 'A diamond is forever' for De Beers when connected to the customers' need for love to be lasting.

CADBURY
DAIRY MILK:
A glass and a half
of milk in
every bar.

GOOGLE:
Its mission is stated
thus: 'to organize the world's
information and make it
universally accessible and useful'.
If they have defined a right to win it would probably be 'algorithms that massively outperform competition that drive user convenience'.

VASANTI:
Its slogan is
'inclusive beauty'.
Its right to win is products that are made to suit all skin colours.

In the example of our fictitious Seatown pizzeria, the offer of pizzas that are fully customizable by customers, including children, would be its right to win.

The company culture

By this I mean the real culture, not the nonsense that is typically inscribed in stone in reception or on the website. This is most often, in my experience, the management's wishful thinking related to the organization's shortcomings. Getting to the bottom of the real culture is a great place to start for organizations that deliver a service or have a very large customer-facing aspect. The culture of the company will strongly affect who they hire, how workers develop and, therefore, what the customer encounters when they meet their staff. In some cases, this is very actively driven as part of the brand. Interestingly, company cultures are often firmly rooted in the founding ethos or origins. Cadbury, a company started by a benevolent Quaker family who built the model village of Bournville, including social housing and a community for its workers, still very much has generosity in its culture. Notwithstanding the acquisition by Mondelez, this value is still at the heart of the brand today.

At Vodafone UK, customers could not touch or feel our product, the mobile network. They noticed our product most when it went wrong. They were most likely to form their views of us by the people they met: our colleagues in our retail stores, or one to one with sales managers in the enterprise division, or when they rang our call centres. Because people were such a large part of our connection with the customer, I looked at the company culture to find our right to win when I was figuring out our brand strategy.

Vodafone began life as RACAL, makers of naval radios, and when I explored its values and culture by interviewing colleagues it was obvious that military values prevailed. My human-resources colleague described the company at its best as follows: 'We are at our best when we have a mountain to climb. We come together, and there may be muck and bullets on the floor by the time we've finished, but we get it done.' The muck and bullets metaphor astounded me, but it was very revealing. I realized that quite a few successful staff were ex-military (including the global and UK CEOs), the organization tended to be hierarchical and junior staff often obeyed instructions without question. This could have its comedy moments, but the culture was unequivocally military. Everywhere I looked there were manifestations of it. There was a memorial garden for our 'fallen heroes' in the grounds of our Newbury HQ, to commemorate those who had died at work, such as falling off masts. There was tremendous 'esprit de corps', a succeed-at-all-costs approach to projects (war is very 'do or die'), a lack of blame culture, and great kindness shown to individuals who fell ill owing to pressure of work, who were described in the language of the fallen.

In order to uncover the most positive expression of this, I looked at archetypes in literature. Storytelling archetypes are a useful tool to help define brands, excellently explained in *The Hero and the Outlaw* (2001) by Margaret Mark and Carol S. Pearson. Military heroes pop up a lot in literature and film and this gave me inspiration. Vodafone staff exhibited archetypal hero behaviours and beliefs. But I had identified that the customer was in a state of dependency regarding their connectivity (see Chapter 9), and this felt a potentially awkward match with a provider that was a military hero. Both were true, but how could

I connect them? Then I looked at the qualities of heroes and realized that 'strength' would be incredibly relevant. It was true of us as a company in many ways (ethics, longevity, financial performance) and had the advantage of being the way mobile phone networks are often described – 'strong signals'. We were also investing heavily in technology to improve the performance of our network, with commitments made for the following three years. So I knew this was a truth for the brand that would not melt away. I articulated this as follows: 'Vodafone is Strong: with a strong network, strong ethics and products and services you can count on'.

I had decided to differentiate Vodafone from our competition, which tended to adopt playful personas and which had been invented from mergers – EE, O2, Three (unlike Vodafone, which had always been Vodafone), by choosing to present ourselves in a more serious way. I summarized this as being a brand of Substance (see Chapter 9). Then, combining the right to win and differentiation crisply together, I described us thus: 'Vodafone is a brand of Strength and Substance.' This was of particular relevance to the enterprise or B2B division of the company, which accounted for half of our revenue and included major corporations, most of the emergency services, most government departments and VIP customers. Certain contracts were so important that even some members of the board were not allowed to know who they were! From call centres to shop floors to directors in charge of major contracts, 'Strength and Substance' stuck in the minds of everyone and, as importantly, it resonated with them. And it needed to. They are the brand, as far as the customer is concerned.

What the company believes in

The core offer or the 'right to win' can be belief-based, although it is more usual for this to come out in the overall theme. Brands with a purpose can be very successful, as we shall discuss in Chapter 11.

Although famously secretive about the components of their strategy, Apple are probably a great example of this, with their strong beliefs about design. Steve Jobs's relentless fixation on having 'one button' led to the mould-breaking iPhone. It is stated that their core belief used to be 'people with passion can change

Jungian archetypes helped us focus Vodafone's right to win and heroic values.

Archetype	Motivation	Motto	Core desire
Creator	Stability & control	If it can be imagined, it can be created.	Create something of enduring value
Caregiver	Stability & control	Love your neighbour as yourself.	Protect people from harm.
Ruler	Stability & control	Power isn't everything. It's the only thing.	Control
Jester	Belonging & enjoyment	If I can't dance, I don't want to be part of your revolution.	To live in the moment with full enjoyment
Regular gal/guy	Belonging & enjoyment	All men and women are created equal.	Connection with others
Lover	Belonging & enjoyment	I only have eyes for you.	Attain intimacy and experience sexual pleasure
Hero	Risk & mastery	Where there's a will, there's a way.	To prove one's worth through courageous and difficult action
Outlaw	Risk & mastery	Rules are meant to be broken.	Revenge or revolution
Magician	Risk & mastery	It can happen!	Knowledge of the fundamental laws of how the world or universe works
Innocent	Independence & fulfilment	Free to be you and me.	To experience paradise
Explorer	Independence & fulfilment	Don't fence me in.	The freedom to find out who you are by exploring the world
Sage	Independence & fulfilment	The truth will set you free.	The discovery of truth

the world for the better', which manifested itself as 'Think different' in the early days of the company. Their current strategies are not public, but their right to win could be 'total commitment to design that customers can use intuitively'. That the iPad needs no instruction manual whatsoever is an outstanding manifestation of this belief and its delivery.

The success of Cisco, a B2B technology conglomerate, is underpinned by 'a belief in the power of connection to achieve what's possible, for customers, partners, employees and the world'. This was its founding ethos, after two Stanford University computer scientists found they could not connect the networks in two different departments and created a local area network, or LAN, to do so. It is still the ethos that underpins the company today, with $52 billion in revenues and 75,000 employees.

If you are in a business that has been around a while and are trying to figure out this right to win, my best advice is to look at what made the brand or company great in the first place. Whether it's the founding beliefs, the culture or something at the heart of the product or service, you will probably find brand gold if you dig there.

If you are in a business that has been around a while, look at what made the brand or company great in the first place

Steve Jobs's legendary commitment to intuitive functionality resulted in mould-breaking 'one button' user interaction and exquisite design.

CHAPTER 8

Connecting your brand to the wider world

Brand strategies up to the second half of the 20th century were built in a context of relatively low levels of competition and a manufacturer-led view of the world. As competition hotted up, figuring out why customers might buy your product or service and how it was different helped. Many brands also began to grasp that their customers were not operating in a vacuum where their lives revolved around the category in which the brand operated. In the early part of the 21st century, savvy marketers realized that a connection with the broader cultural context provided opportunities to allow the brands to stand for something bigger, as well as more scope for PR and partnerships. And then social media kicked in, which was transformational. Brands that had figured out that they had a relevant role in something bigger going on in the world could legitimately engage with the dialogue that was happening on the various social media platforms. It's a tricky one for brands to get right, and, unfortunately, recent history is littered with brands that have been clumsy or got above themselves in this regard. Success comes from being both humble and ambitious. It's rare, but some brands have risen to that challenge.

How to use context in brand strategy
Before considering this aspect, I recommend that the work on customer insight, the right to win and the differentiation is considered first (see Chapters 5, 6 and 7). This will give vital

understanding of how the brand matters or could matter to the customer. This fourth lever of the brand strategy framework I like, cultural context, is best considered last. To uncover yours, look at trends that have relevance or connection to the customer and to the area of operation for the brand. You need to check two things: that the trend does have an impact on your customer (and get data to support it if possible), and that it is a trend that appears to be growing over a fairly long period, which will give your brand strategy longevity. Avoid fads. Eating healthily is a long-term trend; the latest diet is most likely a fad. That way your strategy will be relevant and built to last.

Avoid fads. That way your strategy will be relevant and built to last.

For example, if you were developing a brand strategy for an app offering investment products for millennials, you would look at trends in their attitudes to money, their expectations for the future, their attitudes to inheritance, their levels of trust in institutions – that sort of thing. Our Seatown pizzeria could look at a number of options: the rise of veganism, allergies, orthorexia (an obsessive preoccupation with eating the right food, however you choose to define it) and other dietary strictures; how families often don't eat together any more in daily life; the role of eating out in society; how holidays are evolving and changing. Having established that it is relevant and has longevity, you then just have to pick one and go with it. There is no right answer, just one that could fit and help your brand connect seamlessly with something bigger. For Seatown, I'd choose the explosion of food needs and demands.

Once a brand has its theme, it can then choose to actively commentate in the press and on social media feeds that relate to the cultural context. This benefits the brand not only by giving it publicity but also by enhancing its relevance. For example, when a magazine or newspaper ran an article on positive body images or on eating disorders, the journalist would often seek a comment from the PR team on Dove at Unilever. At Vodafone, we would engage with the issues of trust around big companies and tech by interacting with such sites as Mumsnet regarding child safety online.

In some cases, this lever will play a very large part in the brand's strategy and in others its contribution will be more subtle. What follows are some examples including brands that I have worked on, examining how this aspect was brought to life.

Dove

For Dove, the cultural context was a major driver of what we did. We identified the pressure to conform to beauty ideals as a major trend, prevalent worldwide. Ogilvy often uncovered regional beauty stereotypes by looking at the most popular corrective surgery in different countries. In Japan, many women have no crease in their eyelid between brow and lash, a feature some dislike and may surgically correct, so a 'single eyelid' was not deemed beautiful. We discovered that beauty ideals varied by country. For example, in Brazil, tightly curled hair was called 'feet in the kitchen hair', a racist epithet implying that the person had slave ancestry. However, in every culture, women worried about being old or too fat. A press headline describing a former member of the British Royal Family in the UK as 'The Duchess of Pork' demonstrates how insidious and nasty media pressure can be. Beauty stereotypes everywhere were pervasive and had existed for generations, and we saw no sign that the pressure to conform was reducing. Kate Winslet had just decried GQ magazine for elongating and slimming her legs on their cover shot of her. In fact, this practice was so normal for magazines that the editor hadn't even considered it necessary to consult her.

When I did a magazine interview in Slovenia about the Dove campaign as it was launching there, the journalist asked if I thought the Virgin Mary was the first example of an unattainable female stereotype! I was completely lost for words on that one, but it's clear that the pressure on women to conform to an ideal is a centuries-old phenomenon. When we launched the campaign social media did not exist, but digital manipulation of images in magazines was having a real impact on women. Since then, social media seems to have made this worse, with huge pressure on young women to conform, and invasive procedures to enhance appearance becoming normalized. So this cultural context is an example of one that is relevant and long-lasting. When we picked it almost 20 years ago, I don't think we had any real idea how much worse it would get.

Interestingly, this is being further developed for the brand with their range for men, branded Dove Men + Care: recently they have challenged male stereotypes and championed the caring role men play by taking a position on paternity leave.

Cultural context is not the same thing as brand purpose

We pioneered the notion of 'brand purpose' with Dove. It was 'Honest Beauty', a theme that connected the insight, the cultural context, the brand's right to win and its differentiation. It is important that brands don't just align themselves with a cultural trend and claim to stand for (or against) that issue – they need to connect the dots to ensure they avoid a disconnect. We did it well and we did it right with Dove and it has lasted and built the brand. Many other companies since then have adopted brand purpose as part of the essential thinking on brands. Like many things, its success, unfortunately, has bred some really bad examples, causing some to discredit the notion of brand purpose. Bad marketing should certainly be discredited, but that doesn't mean the underlying principles should be.

Some would suggest that brand purpose should be replaced with circular economics, this being the state where brands have no environmental footprint. When this is accomplished, of course, it will make the world a better place, but it is not going to create any differentiation for brands. Hopefully, all brands will eventually make no environmental impact and it will become a hygiene factor. Forgive the pun, but in my view low or no environmental impact is not a sustainable brand positioning. Maybe if you establish a reputation for zero carbon footprint ahead of anyone else, and continue to go beyond this, perhaps by regenerating the environment in some way, it might be a positioning that will last. It could form the cultural context for a brand, but the brand theme will still have to connect it to the customer insight, right to win and differentiation.

When it comes to selecting your cultural context, the key is to make absolutely sure that the issue you are choosing to engage with has an effect on your customer and that your brand has good connection with it.

> **Make absolutely sure that the issue you are choosing to engage with has an effect on your customer and that your brand has good connection with it.**

Milka

As detailed in Chapter 5, we identified that people soothed themselves with milk chocolate to better connect with their loved ones, and we planned to differentiate by being a social brand rather than an escapist, indulgent one. So we looked for global trends in family life and the causes of stresses and strains, and realized that there were long-term, intractable changes that were putting more pressure on families: for example divorce, remarriage or moving for work. I recall that we defined this as 'families and friends in fluid motion, struggling with connection'. Our advertising featured scenes in which our icon, the lilac Milka cow, nudged people in family situations to be closer together when they were holding back from being loving to one another. Some countries' brand communication encouraged people to challenge local customs, such as keeping your distance from neighbours. As a humble bar of chocolate, we didn't go in guns blazing commenting on political or social issues, but this context influenced our advertising very strongly.

Airbnb

This brand is underpinned by values of community-led and culturally diverse travel. Their offer has always leveraged the insight that customers want to feel a sense of belonging when they travel. So when there were some accusations of discriminatory behaviour by hosts in 2017, Airbnb came out fighting with a moving rebuttal in a TV commercial called 'We accept', in which they stated: 'We believe no matter who you are, where you're from, who you love or who you worship, we all belong. We all believe that the world is more beautiful the more you accept. #weaccept'. And again in 2018, after the USA imposed travel restrictions on foreign nationals visiting from five Muslim majority countries, they responded with 'Let's keep travelling forward', a commercial that points out that travel and migration underpin the very fabric of the USA.

Airbnb don't use my framework to define their brand strategy, but if they did, the cultural context they were leveraging and engaging with would be that of diversity, both its tensions and its advantages. If I had to fill out my framework, I'd put: 'People everywhere can feel challenged by the differences they encounter as people migrate and merge in the world.' And because this is consistent with their brand offer and the insight that their customers want a sense of belonging, when they do step out publicly on issues, it feels natural and the right thing to do. Without that anchor in strategy, they could get shouty on all sorts of topics, but they don't. It builds the brand and adds to the good in the world. What better definition of brand purpose than that?

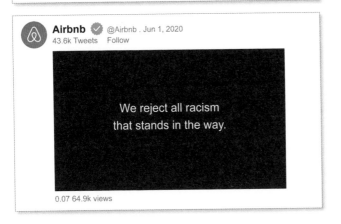

Social media engagement provides opportunities for a brand to express its core values.

Pick a context, any context

No! A brand cannot have any context it likes. If you randomly grab a social issue and try to graft it on to your brand, then you are likely to be discredited by the public, who will recognize it for the opportunistic tactic that it is.

I was baffled by a Christmas TV commercial that ran in 2014 in the UK for the mass-market supermarket Sainsbury's, which celebrated the brief 'Christmas truce' that occurred in the trenches during the First World War. This mythologized event involved soldiers from the UK and Germany stopping shooting, singing carols and exchanging presents around the time of Christmas. It was a moving and poignant moment in history, and I encourage you to research it. Sainsbury's were selling a bar of chocolate for the British Legion, a charity that supports veterans, and 2014 marked 100 years since the start of the Great War. The head of brand communications said it celebrated sharing at Christmas. But for a supermarket whose strapline is 'Live well for less' the Christmas truce seemed to me to be an entirely random choice of event, and utterly unconnected with

No! A brand cannot have any context it likes.

anything the brand had stood for to date. It felt more opportunistic than sincere.

And then there is the subject itself, outside of any brand strategy issues. The *Guardian*, a well-respected upmarket British newspaper, described the ad as a 'dangerous and disrespectful masterpiece', feeling that it made a hideous war look beautiful and exploited it for commercial gain. And I can't help wondering how much it cost to shoot the film and how much the charity received as a donation from the chocolate sales. Even allowing for the charitable angle, I probably wouldn't accept that the end justified the means.

So beware if you take on a serious issue as a brand. Pepsi waded into the Black Lives Matter movement in 2017, with a TV commercial featuring fashion model Kendall Jenner joining young, diverse protesters and handing a police officer a can of Pepsi. In response, the crowd in the commercial cheer wildly. Not so enthusiastic the response of the public and the media. Described as possibly the worst ad of all time, it created a huge backlash, was rapidly withdrawn and was followed by an apology by Pepsi. Again, my feeling is that, unlike Airbnb, which have publicly championed inclusion and whose values are rooted there, this soda brand does not have diversity at its core. It has spent many years investing in taking on Coca-Cola with taste challenges. And it did not really know its place in this sensitive subject, overreaching itself in its portrayal of the soft drink as a bringer of peace between protesters and law enforcement. Funnily enough, I think Coca-Cola might have pulled this off, with its history including one of the most iconic TV commercials of all time, 'I'd like to teach the world to sing'.

Brand owners do need to believe in their brand but also can so easily forget themselves and think they are more important than they are. Humility and empathy are core skills for CMOs and brand directors, but I've never found either on any of their job descriptions.

CHAPTER 9

What does your brand have to offer overall?

This is the most exciting bit: the brand theme. Other frameworks call it the 'brand essence' or 'brand idea'. Whatever it's called, it's the short sharp summation of what the brand is all about and is where all the other analysis and thinking leads. It will drive everything you do in the longer term. It is the main thing about your brand that customers will play back to you in their own words. The reason I prefer 'theme' as opposed to 'essence' or 'idea' is because some brands, especially those with complex structures or multiple products, may need to vary their messages accordingly. A theme can unite all aspects and represent the brand in all its dimensions. 'Brand essence' may be more limiting or one-dimensional, and 'brand idea' makes it feel too communication or advertising oriented, whereas this is a strategic concept for all aspects of marketing. Whether or not you like my choice of approach, this summation is the most important part of a brand's strategy. It should be short, single-minded and memorable, expressed in very few words – probably not more than ten. It's not the same as the slogan which should derive from that strategic thought, of course, but should have a bit more pizzazz and sometimes isn't as explicit.

It should be short, single-minded and memorable.

In more traditional marketing, the leading thought about a brand would have been defined as the customer benefit – what the customer gained from the product or service. As stated in Chapter 3, this approach is a little simplistic in today's competitive and hyperconnected world. A benefit would typically link the customer need or insight to what the product delivered, for example:

Insight:
Women start to worry about ageing when they hit 40.

Insight:
It's hard to tell fact from fiction when booking a hotel because there is so much PR involved.

Brand proposition:
iCream reduces the appearance of fine lines and wrinkles.

or:

Brand proposition:
We filter your priorities and profile but don't filter the reviews.

Brand benefit:
No one need ever know your age.

Brand benefit:
Reviews you can count on.

In my four levers model, differentiation and cultural context levers are factored in and this leads to something more interesting. For these same examples:

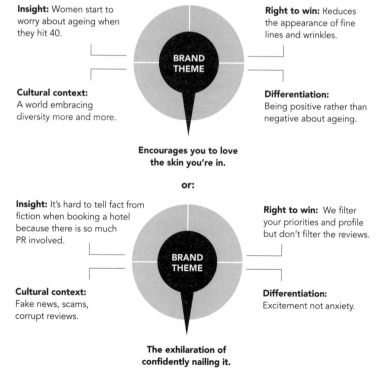

Insight: Women start to worry about ageing when they hit 40.

Right to win: Reduces the appearance of fine lines and wrinkles.

BRAND THEME

Cultural context:
A world embracing diversity more and more.

Differentiation:
Being positive rather than negative about ageing.

Encourages you to love the skin you're in.

or:

Insight: It's hard to tell fact from fiction when booking a hotel because there is so much PR involved.

Right to win: We filter your priorities and profile but don't filter the reviews.

BRAND THEME

Cultural context:
Fake news, scams, corrupt reviews.

Differentiation:
Excitement not anxiety.

The exhilaration of confidently nailing it.

Some I did earlier: Dove

The strategy for Dove that became the idea 'Real Beauty' took over a year to figure out. (Then getting the ad campaign right took a further full year.) It was an intelligent and thoughtful, if meandering, journey. This is the story of what actually happened. Our thinking was radical at the time and it became the model for the new paradigm of 'purpose-led' branding. In hindsight, how we thought about it very much fitted with the framework I have come to love for figuring out brands. But we didn't have a guide at the time and despite the way the story of the campaign is told in business schools and universities – as an example of paradigm shifting and world-class marketing, where it looks like the seamless logic of a bunch of geniuses – it was much more of a muddle that felt as if we were just grappling with our ambition to do something world-class.

We started by identifying Dove's values. We did this by reviewing all the ad campaigns it had done since its launch in the 1950s to identify what resonated with us and what was successful with the customer. One TV commercial stood out. It was a 'testimonial' that ran in the 1980s in the USA, featuring a woman very different from the archetypal beauty of the day. Bo Derek, Cheryl Tiegs or other white, blonde, leggy models generally featured on the covers of magazines and in ads back then; the star of our TV commercial, Jean Shy, was curvy, Black and with a gossipy, mischievous character. In the commercial, she told a story of flirting with her pastor about how lovely her skin was. This was very transgressive in many ways at that time. Another woman also inspired us, Sato-san, the star of a Dove TV testimonial in Japan, who was the antithesis of the demure and dainty women more commonly seen there. As a pattern emerged, we realized that 'realness' was a big part of the brand's success. We selected a small number of core values that defined the brand, including 'real', 'timeless' and 'optimistic'.

As a pattern emerged, we realized that 'realness' was a big part of the brand's success.

But it was realness, more than all of the other values, that made us really stand out from our competitors. When we looked at other brands, they were all using skinny, mostly teenage models, retouched to within an inch of their lives, looking as though they were more in need of a good lunch than of whichever unguent they were promoting. We realized that these images made most of the women on the strategy team at the time feel pretty inadequate, and we discovered the true impact of the usual representation of beauty on women by consulting with psychologists and finding other academic studies. It was proved that looking at beauty magazines lowered women's self-esteem, measured by science. We had our insight: the beauty industry makes women feel ugly.

And it was clear that matters were getting worse and worse, with the ease of digital retouching making image manipulation more accessible, and with the rise and rise of cosmetic surgery.

Dove four levers model applied to Dove.

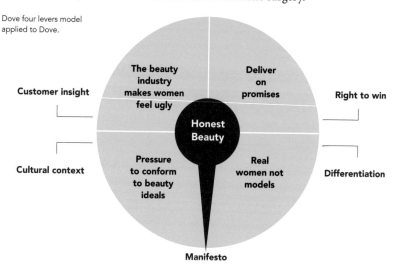

These Dove ads ask readers to question beauty ideals. Half empty or half full? Grey or gorgeous?

We drew these themes together into our 'brand essence' – 'Beauty without Artifice'. Once our mould-breaking ad campaign was in the public domain, and we had aligned our theme with a product strategy, we felt confident enough to move to the bolder and more positive theme of 'Honest Beauty'.

The first advertising expressing this 'essence' was launched in 2004, 'The Campaign for Real Beauty', which surprised and delighted the world. The concept of 'real beauty' also directed the launch of products such as 'Pro Age', as opposed to the anti-ageing products that are typically offered to women. It also inspired the removal of 'emotive ingredients', which are those ingredients that are commonly promoted in beauty products but are contained in such small quantities that they do not account for the product's performance as implied. Beauty, sadly, is not a very honest category, and we decided to hold ourselves to higher standards. Nowadays, Dove ads still celebrate Real Women and Real Beauty (although without the 'Campaign' slogan) and their product ranges generally don't fib about ingredients. Two decades on, Honest Beauty is still going strong and building the brand.

Some I did earlier: Milka

At Mondelez, the global team had developed a framework involving inputs that inspired the ones I use today. Milka was a brand I was responsible for and whose 'four box' brand strategy I co-created with a small number of brilliant colleagues. The work we did became the example that demonstrated best-practice use of the 'four box' framework. My only issue with it was that there were seven boxes in it. The customer insight we gained for Milka came from the ethnographic research we did with customers in five countries – Russia, Serbia, Poland, Germany and France – as described in Chapter 5. This revealed that people had a role in their lives for milk chocolate which was probably subconscious and unlocked a wonderful new idea for the brand. We discovered that milk chocolate enabled adults to be nicer to those they loved because it soothed their nerves.

We had realized that we could stand out by focusing on 'we' not 'me'.

Many competitor brands at the time tended to focus on 'me time' or self-indulgence, which represented the self-soothing part to some degree but which missed the point of it all – the connecting better with the ones they loved. We had realized that we could stand out by focusing on 'we' not 'me'. And this insight on how much family, friends and loved ones mattered to our customers and how we could connect it all together for our brand was really exciting.

What also excited us was that the effect felt by consumers was actually true of chocolate. Not only does milky sweetness soothe, but theobromine, an active ingredient of cocoa, is a lifter of mood.

We also recognized that the global context was making connecting more challenging. Megatrends everywhere were: divorce, remarriage, recombining families, people moving away to work, sometimes overseas, more and more families relying on two workers to stay afloat. We summed this up as 'families and friends in fluid motion'. This context would enable a broader relevance for the brand and offer up potential PR stories and relevant ideas for brand activity. Linking this together, we realized

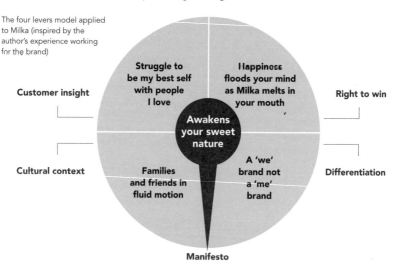

The four levers model applied to Milka (inspired by the author's experience working for the brand)

Customer insight

Cultural context

Right to win

Differentiation

Struggle to be my best self with people I love

Happiness floods your mind as Milka melts in your mouth

Awakens your sweet nature

Families and friends in fluid motion

A 'we' brand not a 'me' brand

Manifesto

Lila, Milka's brand icon, became the star of our TV commercials, daring people to be 'a little more tender'.

that 'Awakens your sweet nature' summed it up and was an idea that could last for Milka.

Some I did earlier: Vodafone

At Vodafone UK, the strategy was developed when smartphones were owned by only 55 per cent of the population. It was evident that people were relying on them more and more to manage and optimize their life. To understand the customer a little more deeply, I looked at academic papers on how people related to their smartphones and at some customer videos, and talked to call centre staff about how customers felt when they lost their phones. Academic papers had discovered that the centres in the brain for 'love and compassion' lit up when people engaged with their smartphones. One of our customer videos involved a little girl with a pink phone, who was asked how a day without her phone would feel and replied 'it would be like a hole in my heart'. Our call centre staff described many customers crying or shouting when they had lost their phones. I realized that customers' relationships with their phones were highly emotional. They were dependent, not only practically but emotionally. And Vodafone's business customers, for whom we provided both mobile and fixed-line systems, had been dependent on telephony for years.

I defined this insight as follows: 'I cannot live, love or work without my phone. I am dependent on it.' The notion of dependency needed to be dramatized for my colleagues and made more attractive to them as a concept. I used an extreme metaphor to evoke their empathy and understanding. Rather as teams in businesses sometimes look at Formula One pit crew to understand teamwork, I chose caring for people with physical dependencies, as a metaphor to bring customer dependency to life. I researched it to empathize with and understand some of the typical feelings of physically dependent individuals and how they wanted their supporters and carers to think and behave to do their job well.

I had identified the hero character archetype as one that defined the culture at Vodafone, as described in Chapter 7. I then figured out what aspects of a hero could appeal to someone who was dependent, again considering the understanding I had gained regarding caring for people with severe paralysis. Strength emerged as a key quality that appealed. I liked it because it included the physical, the emotional and the ethical. And the icing on the cake was that people describe a good mobile signal as a strong one. Strength would be very relevant to a state of dependency. Being dependent on something flaky or weak is not a good experience, and potentially even frightening. And I felt that strength would appeal to my colleagues as a characteristic.

Looking at our differentiation, competitors were playful in their manner, with jokey, cool or whimsical advertising and personas. We needed to be different, and I felt that a provider that was more serious would also be welcomed by that dependent customer. 'Serious' seemed a bit too sober and not a motivating factor for our British staff, so I chose the term 'substance' instead. This would enable us to have a sense of humour, but we would stand out from our lighthearted competitors. If you were dependent, wouldn't you prefer your provider to be of substance, not a joker?

Last came the general external context. In the UK we were just emerging from a series of corporate scandals involving much-loved institutions such as the BBC; we had been treated to horsemeat in our lasagne by some trusted food brands; and demonstrators were chaining themselves to HQ buildings to protest against companies that they believed were paying insufficient tax. The public were losing faith in big organizations and big business. I chose this thought to be the cultural context to mitigate the darker side of the hero archetype. The hero's weakness is arrogance, and I wanted the brand to serve, not save, the customer. I felt that the public would prefer to hear from customers rather than from a big corporation. I didn't want Vodafone to toot its own horn, as was its tendency. I used the context to define the appropriate sort of hero to colleagues at Vodafone – a humble hero, with an 'all in the line of duty, ma'am' style, as opposed to someone on a podium with medals. When we developed advertising, we shone a spotlight on our customers and let them tell their own stories.

Their voices were heard more than Vodafone's.

So how do you pull these things together and make a single thought? Again, I drew on my understanding of people with disabilities for inspiration. They would want to be empowered and elevated and they would want their life to be the best and boldest possible.

Customers were getting more out of life from their phones… being more, doing more. I felt this could be summarized as:

'Vodafone sustains people's bolder lives.' The choice of words was important, especially the word 'people's'. I was worried, with our tendency to arrogance, that we would take too much credit, and people could quickly subvert this into meaning that Vodafone would make them bolder. This would not be what people wanted to hear! We needed instead to celebrate our customers and know our place – to help them go where they wanted to go, not to make them better human beings. Again, our insight into people with physical disabilities helped: I learned that two things wheelchair users cannot stand are people moving their wheelchairs, and people not sitting down when they talk to them, putting them at eye level and therefore on equal terms. Extrapolating from this, we knew we had to treat our customers' dependency delicately. And this way of phrasing it made how we should address them and deliver for them much clearer.

When we developed advertising, we shone a spotlight on our customers and let them tell their own stories.

I left Vodafone in summer 2015, and it seems that this strategy was quickly abandoned judging by the advertising that followed. I felt that what we were doing was working, as we had halted and started to reverse a decline in the number of non-Vodafone customers considering us when choosing their next network. As stated in Chapter 3, consistency is a major enabler of brand building, and it saddens me that Vodafone seem unable to build their brand strategies to last.

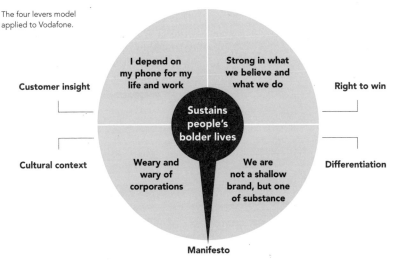

The four levers model applied to Vodafone.

Customer insight — I depend on my phone for my life and work

Right to win — Strong in what we believe and what we do

Sustains people's bolder lives

Cultural context — Weary and wary of corporations

Differentiation — We are not a shallow brand, but one of substance

Manifesto

Other great examples

Of course, the strategic theme drives more than just the ad campaigns, but these are the most public manifestation of their thinking so are good examples to look at. Some other brands whose big ideas and themes have stood the test of time are shown below.

There are many brands that have identified their overall offer and have stuck to it for, well, decades. Brands should resist the urge to chop and change their big themes over time and should invest time in the process to build a strategy that will last. Even more important is the buy-in of the whole leadership. What a brand's theme is to be in the long term should of course be a matter for the CEO and the board, not just the CMO or brand director. If all realized that a brand is the sum of product and reputation, this would not even be questioned. Yet, all too often, a change of marketing director results in a change of strategy. The board of directors should block this sort of thing.

Brands should change their big idea, theme, essence, or whatever you choose to call it, only if it has ceased to be relevant to the customer – not the marketing director.

Brands should resist the urge to chop and change their big themes

A selection of world-class brand offers and slogans.

NIKE

Inspiration to every athlete* in the world.
*If you have a body, you're an athlete.

JUST DO IT

COCA COLA

Refreshment and optimism

open happiness

L'OREAL

Female affirmation

Because you're worth it

DISNEYLAND

Immersive magic

THE HAPPIEST PLACE ON EARTH

SAP

We help the world run better

Best-run businesses run SAP

CHAPTER 10

Crafting your manifesto and socking it to the organization

So far, all the components of a brand strategy have been about crafting crisp thoughts. Shorter is better because it forces choices and single-mindedness, enabling a brand to stand for something clear in the mind of its customer. There then comes a point where you have to expand and elevate this into a poetic story that will inspire your staff and customers. There should be different versions of this narrative for internal and external audiences, but of course they must fit together. If the story is to inspire, it must be meaningful and have a sense of purpose. If you have been in the world of marketing, you will be very aware of 'brand purpose'. For those who have not, this concept has been around for about 20 years. I should know: I was one of the people that invented it with the work on Dove, even if we didn't coin the phrase.

Yet 'brand purpose' has been much debated, derided and defended in recent years. It means a brand standing for something bigger than its features or benefits. Why is the matter so controversial? Many people have confused purpose with virtue, sustainability or ethics, which may be involved, but are not a given. Alternatively, many have selected something purposeful at random and tried to graft it on to the brand without linking it to the brand's strategy. Maybe there was no brand strategy in the first place – an omission much more common than you might think. As a result, some truly dire purpose-led ideas have popped into the world, leading the principle itself to be questioned.

Understood properly and delivered well, it is, without doubt, a brilliant way to build brands.

There are three key matters to understand:

1. Customers like companies to stand for something. Leading PR firm Edelman studied consumers globally in 2018 and found that 64 per cent of consumers chose a brand based upon where it stood on societal or political issues they cared about. China led their league table in this regard, with 78 per cent of customers stating this, with UK (57 per cent) and Germany (54 per cent) being bottom of the eight countries that participated in the survey. Overall, this was 13 per cent higher than the previous year. Accenture found almost identical results in 35 countries, where 62 per cent of 29,530 customers interviewed said they wanted companies to take a stand on issues relevant to the wider world.

64% of consumers chose a brand based upon where it stood on societal or political issues they cared about.

2. Purpose is different from ethics in general. A brand's purpose must be related to what the products or services do, not an add-on. This is where companies have gone wrong. This is also why adopting sustainability as your brand's purpose is risky for brands, because as all organizations will aim to be carbon neutral or to have a circular economy model, this position will be difficult to retain as a differentiator. For example, a brand can have a purpose related to bringing beauty to the world or championing radical design, yet still be as ethical as, or more ethical than, the next company. Customers do care about ethics, in fact more and more, but as one of my old bosses used to say, 'customers hire a brand to do a job for them', and therefore doing that job is the most relevant thing. If what the brand does for the customer has an ethical dimension as well, then that's the holy grail.

3. Purpose does not need to be virtuous to build a brand. In their seminal book on corporate strategy, *Built to Last* (1994), Jim Collins and Jerry I. Porras demonstrate that companies that stand for something outperform their competitive equivalents in stock market returns by a factor of seven in the long term. A big driver of that performance is the discretionary effort delivered by staff because they believe in the thing that the organization stands for. They

cite as an example tobacco company Philip Morris, one of
the businesses in their study, which identified a purpose in
standing for freedom, thereby tacitly allowing the public to
do themselves harm if they wanted. Not an area of business
I am at all keen on, but a good way to make this point.
Harley-Davidson's internal positioning statement was at one
time, 'The only motorcycle manufacturer that makes big, loud
motorcycles for macho guys (and "macho wannabes"), mostly
in the United States, who want to join a gang of cowboys, in an
era of decreasing personal freedom.' This manifests itself in
advertising with headlines such as 'Screw it, let's ride' and
'Mainstream. Give it a two-wheel salute.' So, you can be
a badass brand with purpose if you want to, and some iconic
brands like Harley are.

Purpose, done right, does build brands. Unilever state on
their website that they have found that their brands with a social
or environmental purpose grew 69 per cent faster than the rest
of their business.

Unilever state that they have found that their brands with a social or environmental purpose grew 69% faster than the rest of their business.

Some of the above points may seem to conflict, hence the
missteps made and the raging debate. My view is that you need
to find a societal or political issue that connects with what your
brand actually does and then derive your purpose from it. This
is why I have the cultural context in the strategy framework.
Then it's much less likely you are going to get a differentiated
brand benefit with half a pound of disconnected ethics grafted
on. And why you'll write your manifesto at the same time as
your strategy to ensure that your strategy has meaning, purpose
and consistency to the internal and external audiences.

In general, the first version should be written for the staff
and should include some things that help them understand
the customer. Then a much shorter and more relevant version
can be included in the About Us section of a website, on
packaging or in another relevant place.

It's probably best to illustrate a manifesto by way of examples...
and on the following pages are five illustrative examples,
including three that I delivered.

Dove

Dove believes that beauty comes in all shapes and sizes. And that real beauty can be truly stunning.

We believe that feeling beautiful is a good thing and every woman's spirit can be uplifted by liking and caring for herself and creating her own individual style of beauty.

However, today's definition of beauty is too narrow, so most women feel they don't measure up – and some even develop hang-ups as a result. We believe stereotypical images of beauty are harmful and we want to change that.

We resolve to make more women feel beautiful every day by inspiring them to take good care of themselves and presenting a refreshing vision of beauty.

Milka

We prize the power and tender touch of chocolate. We think chocolate is a perfect way to slip into your best self.
Chocolate frees your mind and joy can follow.

We are passionate about the simple way Milka chocolate lifts you up. It's why we make Milka chocolate with a creamy, chocolaty melt that brings about a blissful feeling.

With each piece of Milka, we hope you awaken your sweet nature. We hope you connect to your most easy-going and cheerful self. We fight for that state of mind where laughter comes easily and you twinkle from the inside out.

We believe it can start small – one piece of chocolate, one smile from the inside, that you pass to someone you love – but that it lives in a big way, as innocence, harmony and sweetness in the world.

Vodafone

Vodafone is for those whose lives are a little bit bolder.

We are for people with 'get up and go'. They make things happen in the world around them and keep going even when the going is tough. They enrich their own lives and lift up the lives of those around them.

We are for the lad who gets back on that skateboard. We are for the university student who gets her school pals together every time she visits home. We are for the dad on the touchline cheering on his kid whether he scores or not. We are for the mum who lets her daughter go to the corner store alone for the first time. We are for the senior who finally gets that Harley. We are for the firefighters, the lifeboat volunteers, the ambulance crews, the nurses. We are for the computer programmer who works overtime to keep her company's IT systems running over the holidays. We are for the entrepreneur who has the guts to step off the corporate ladder to build something all his own. We are for the family cycling to Brighton dressed as carrots in memory of the grandfather whose heart gave out too soon.

We salute you, the seizers of life's moments, and we share your view that fortune favours the brave. You inspire us to work hard to make you feel sure of Vodafone's strength and support. So you can be that little bit bolder in what you take on.

Vodafone. Power to you.

SAP

At SAP, our purpose is to help the world run better and improve people's lives. Our promise is to innovate to help our customers run at their best. We engineer solutions to fuel innovation, foster equality, and spread opportunity across borders and cultures.

Being best-run means making a difference.
We are committed to helping every customer become a best-run business. Our global reach enables organizations to achieve meaningful business outcomes to realize both purpose and profit. Through our SAP Purpose Network, we connect people and information to discover solutions to pressing global issues, at scale.

Together, we can transform industries, grow economies, lift up societies, and sustain our environment.

Google

**Google's Ten Things We Know to be True
(in edited form)**
We first wrote 'Ten Things' when Google was a few years old.
From time to time we revisit this list to see if it still holds.
We hope it does and you can hold us to that.

Focus on the user and all else will follow.
It's best to do one thing really, really well.
Fast is better than slow.
Democracy on the web works.
You don't need to be at your desk to need an answer.
You can make money without doing evil.
There's always more information out there.
The need for information crosses all borders.
You can be serious without a suit.
Great just isn't good enough.

Delivering the brand internally

Once you've got all the strategy done and articulated in its most inspiring form, the bad news is that only a fraction of the work is done if you are a large organization. I agree with the oft-quoted success ratio: 10 per cent inspiration, 90 per cent perspiration. That is absolutely the case with establishing brand understanding and execution properly, or 'landing the brand' in any organization with more than 100 or so employees. Many marketers underestimate the effort required to land the brand with the organization, myself included. I've done it well, and I've done it badly. To do it well, involves a serious time, money and energy commitment to ensure that everyone in the company not only gets it but also knows how to implement it. And given that there is always staff turnover in any organization, this is not a one-off task: the communication and education effort need to be continuous.

To do this well, this is what I recommend, having learned from my successes and my mistakes.

A shortened form of Google's long-term manifesto as displayed on their website.

1. Get buy-in from the most senior individual in your company, and get them to send the all-staff announcement about the new brand strategy, with an invitation to come to an event to hear all about it. Not only does this attract people's attention but it immediately raises the status of the brand in the organization. Brand is the combination of the product and reputation, which everyone cares about, but all too often term 'brand' can be relegated to image communications or 'the colouring-in' department and not taken as seriously. If the CEO shows that they believe the brand matters, then it will matter to everyone. As it should.

If the CEO shows that they believe the brand matters, then it will matter to everyone.

2. Invest time and money in the best show-and-tell you can muster. And tailor it to all the stakeholders, from the board to the executive leadership to colleagues in-store and at call centres. I was walking to the in-house theatre one day to present my brand strategy to the umpteenth group of stakeholders with the UK CEO, Jeroen Hoencamp. 'I feel I'm working in showbusiness,' I grumbled. He offered a simple rebuke: 'That's your job!' – and he was 100 per cent right. I never complained again.

The way we landed the strategy for Dove has become something of a legend in the marketing industry. We found a huge difference in the way men and women responded. Women said, 'That's so brilliant! Go sisters!' Men were utterly baffled. When we explained that women almost never thought they were beautiful, men replied, 'But of course you are beautiful, you're women!' When we then added that we did in fact spend significant parts of the day worrying about the size of our asses, we got no further, receiving a dismissive 'But your asses are fine!' response. We realized we had a real problem. Most of the senior leaders at Unilever were men, who would really have to be convinced to adopt such a radical strategy.

We had to figure out a way to make them fall in love with the strategy and commit to it in the way women did. I believed it would have to feel personal for the men in the way it was to women, and suggested that we did short video interviews with their wives or daughters to bring the point home. Silvia Lagnado, the global brand director at Unilever, persuaded the executives' wives to let us interview their daughters in secret, and not one of them split on us to their husbands. Go sisters! The wonderful creative director on Dove at ad agency Ogilvy, Vel Ritchey-Rankin, turned my idea of a video of the girls into a spectacularly moving piece of film. In it, each girl's photo appears, one after the other, alongside a quote about what she doesn't like about her looks. The images are powerfully set to Joe Cocker singing 'You Are So Beautiful (To Me)'. When we met with the senior execs, to conclude our strategy presentation we played this video, and in it, completely unexpectedly, were their very own daughters. People cried. And they approved the strategy. This might be the most shameless example of emotional manipulation in corporate history! I prefer to think of it as a lesson in how to persuade anyone, head and heart. Unilever further invested in a roadshow to take this strategy to the 400 marketers worldwide who work on the brand. This was a significant investment of energy, effort, time and money. Without getting the commitment of the leaders, I think that when we produced the communication about nine months later we would have been stopped in our tracks. It was without question worth every ounce of effort it took. And this brings me to my third piece of advice.

3. Sock the strategy to the whole organization and ensure it is understood by those that have to implement it. The example cited for Dove is exactly what should happen. Unilever is one of the most brand-literate companies on the planet, but even so, energy was invested in further workshops to discuss and torture-test what sort of thing would be on-brand and off-brand.

At Vodafone, I came unstuck at first because I had overestimated the level of my marketing team's experience in executing a new brand strategy. They hadn't had to do this before. And many teams won't have, so it's best to assume they will need guidance. Thankfully, this came home to me early on when we launched our new Customer Experience Centre at our HQ. It had been refurbished to reflect the brand as one of Strength and Substance and I had been heavily involved in its design. On the morning of the launch, I arrived at work to discover that the foyer of our offices had been decorated with giant red bows everywhere with Vodafone-red footprints across the floor leading to the new Experience Centre. It looked like a cross between a Christmas sale at Walmart and the sanguinous footprints from *Die Hard*. I realized that my team would need more coaching on how to execute the new strategy. Bringing to life a new vision is much harder than you ever think it's going to be and needs active involvement from the person with that vision, until there are enough examples to illustrate and guide others in the organization. And time for the teams concerned to understand, practise and be coached on what is on-brand and off-brand. Then let them loose on decorating the foyer!

Bringing to life a new vision needs active involvement from the person with that vision.

Milka was another partial fail for me on landing the brand. The set-up at Mondelez was that my pan-European team delivered the strategy and key communication assets and the individual countries delivered other materials and would send them to me at the HQ in Zurich to see after the event. We created a big launch event in the ski resort of Lech in Austria for all the marketing managers to launch Milka's new strategy. We explained how and why it was changing from the Alpine clichés it had owned (chalets, milk churns, lederhosen, dirndls, blondes with plaits – Heidi on steroids, if you like) to the new theme of 'Awakening your sweet nature' exemplified by the ad campaign 'Dare to be tender'. We explained how much customers loved Lila, the lilac cow, and that she was now going to be key brand asset. Everyone went away clear on how the brand was changing and seemed very positive about it. Sales growth had been lacklustre or flat, but the markets adopting the new strategy typically showed double-digit growth rates. However, even after a decent interval, I continued to receive marketing materials from Germany awash with lederhosen and chalets. I was told it took time for the German team to adopt change, but it would come. After nine months of dirndls, I could stand it no longer and set off for the German HQ in Bremen to find out for myself what was going on. When I took the team through the strategy again, they were amazed and said they thought it was brilliant. They confessed that they had simply not understood it in Lech. Had we had growth rates similar to those we saw in other markets, the additional revenue in a market the size of Germany would have been immense. The impact of this wasted year didn't bear thinking about. I kicked myself, and promised I'd never take full comprehension for granted ever again. The team there were competent, and once they 'got it', tenderness ruled. And I was lederhosen-free from then on.

So as someone wise once said to me, if you want something to happen when people are involved, (or to get to the bottom of why something isn't happening), you need to ask three questions: 'Do they know what to do? Can they do it? Do they want to do it?' I think the only time that all three bits of magic came together brilliantly was for Dove. With other brands, some bits were missing and remedies were needed.

4. Integrate brand strategy understanding into the business-as-usual company inductions and training. At Vodafone, I created a new team whose role it was to take the brand roadshow to our 12,000 employees – and thousands of colleagues had been exposed to it by the time I left. It was presented by one of my team at all new starters' inductions. In addition, I created an online training tool by which customer-facing staff learned to better understand the customer and how we were delivering the brand. Lush, which regularly wins awards for customer service, is famous for training its staff, in my view superbly connecting service with the brand's sustainability principles by demonstrating how selling the customer the right product avoids waste.

5. Lastly, the landing of a brand strategy and ensuring its consistent execution is a continuous job, like painting the Golden Gate Bridge. People in any organization change, and the new ones need to be brought on board; and you learn how to deliver the brand better and better as time goes on. So you'll find more and more examples of best practice that will require you to update and refine how you execute the strategy. These will sometimes inspire you to polish up the strategy a bit, too, as we did with taking Dove from 'Beauty without Artifice' to 'Honest Beauty'.

A brand director's work is never done and a big part of it is showbiz.

In all of this, the thing to know is that a brand director's work is never done and a big part of it is showbiz. And I am ever grateful to a blunt Dutchman, Jeroen, for pointing this out.

Part 2: Execution

This is the stuff that everyone loves. Bringing a strategy to life is the best thing in the world. No customer buys a PowerPoint deck. While figuring out a strategy is time well spent and will make all the difference to the end result, it counts for naught if the brilliant thinking doesn't make it into the real world.

This second section of the book outlines the key areas where a brand strategy will need to be brought to life in order to move it from theory to reality. Its purpose is to guide you through the impact of the different pillars of building a brand, illustrated mostly by good but also by some bad and ugly ways that brands have been built or harmed.

How do you move to the execution stage?

Converting a strategy into reality is easier said than done. Do you do a lot of stuff in theory? Or do you get going, 'moving fast and breaking things', to use a phrase so popular in the digital community? I believe you need to do a bit of both, but err on the side of the fast-moving model.

My recommendation would be to get started with only one or two things designed in theory. There is nothing like the white heat of reality to encourage high standards and practicality, and doing too much without a certain amount of pressure can often result in things that then have to be undone or redone later.

Unless you work in a very small organization or start-up, you will need to deliver your strategy through other people across the organization, many of whom probably won't report to you if you are the CMO or brand director. But individuals across an organization often don't understand things in the abstract: you will need to bring the strategy to life with examples, so they begin to see how it works in practice. How brand-literate your organization is will determine how many examples they may need to see to 'get it'. These are also the individuals who will deliver or even manifest the brand themselves, and getting their thoughts at an early stage will not only be instructive but also help to get them on board. A series of consultative meetings with key stakeholder groups would be a great way to get their input on how to begin to execute and might even modify the strategy itself. However, a word of caution: any creative endeavour is rarely great if delivered by a committee, so ensure the meetings are about how to implement the strategy, not how to hone it into mediocrity by many individuals worrying away at it.

The recent explosion of new opportunities to bring a strategy to life across new channels and technologies has made this even more exciting than ever and one of the reasons why being a brand director or CMO is fascinating and exciting no matter which industry you work in. The execution of a brand's strategy involves being in a constant state of test and learn.

Job done then?

When you move into the execution of a new strategy, the last thing the CMO, brand director or business owner must do is let go. That can happen once most of the key elements have been delivered. Until this is the case, they need to stay all over it until it is done. You will find as you go that elements of the strategy will need refinement or you may uncover even better ways to express things. Real life is scrappy, and this journey often isn't an easy one. Great brand directors need to be almost psychopathically committed to bringing the vision of their strategy to life, but humble enough to correct course when the theory just can't be made to work in practice.

The second half of the book also highlights how you can go about getting the execution adopted and how you create assets to maintain it.

I hope the examples in this part of the book bring the theory to life for you and inspire you to the degree of doggedness it takes to bring a great brand strategy to your customers.

CHAPTER 11

What should your brand be called?

Naming a brand is probably one of the most important decisions you can take. Naming a totally new brand doesn't happen in the lifetime of most corporate brand directors; naming new products, however, is much more commonplace. I've named several new products, but only two new brands and those were start-ups. If you're starting a business from scratch, it will probably be one of the first things you do and it's likely that you'll do it before you've even figured out the strategy for your business. Which is the wrong way round – but is normally what happens.

The name can enhance the appeal of your business significantly, so it's better done once you have a strategy, but you shouldn't be afraid to change the name really quickly if you think you've made a mistake. Many business owners can't bring themselves to do this, but there is absolutely no harm in doing so if not much awareness and reputation has been established. Jeff Bezos changed the name of his company three times in the first year of business – from Cadabra to Relentless to Amazon. It was a long journey to get to Sony for its founder, Masaru Ibuka. It started as Tokyo Tsushin Kyogo, difficult outside its home market. He considered TTK and Tokyo Teltech but they were in use by other companies; and Totsuko, a contraction of the full name, was still a struggle for Westerners.

Consumer brands suffer most from name changes, although B2B brands suffer less because their customers are typically more engaged and may well be retained by contracts. You'll be

Jeff Bezos changed the name of his company three times in the first year of business.

in good company if you switch brand names, but do it quickly, as there is a price to be paid if you've already built any awareness and reputation.

Cautionary tales from history

Those of a sensitive disposition might want to skip this section, as it contains 'adult themes'. There are many popular videos on YouTube poking fun at food products from non-English-speaking countries that are called things like Urinal, Cemen Dip and Pee Cola. Unless any of these manufacturers have ambitions to expand into English-speaking countries, I see nothing wrong with any of these names if they work for the intended customers in their home country. They are not 'hilarious fails' in my view.

More deserving of a good snicker are those where globally distributed companies have tripped up. For example, Honda launched its small hatchback as the Fitta, before quickly renaming it the Jazz, having discovered *fitta* is a vulgar word for female genitals in Nordic countries. *Siri* means 'cock' in Georgian, *latte* is slang for 'erection' in German and *sega* is Italian slang for 'masturbate'.

More sensibly, Mitsubishi named its Pajeros SUV differently in different regions, avoiding the name sounding like the slang for someone 'playing with himself' in Spanish by dubbing it the Montero in countries where Spanish is spoken. It's called the Shogun in the UK for some reason. Presumably a Spanish-sounding product from a Japanese motor company was more than the Brits could handle.

Finding a name that is meaningful and has no unfortunate connotations anywhere in the world is much harder than it looks. When Kraft renamed its snack division Mondelez, it did a lot of due diligence and crowd-sourced ideas for the name from its employees. The new name was launched to great fanfare simultaneously in every country in the world where Kraft traded. A few days later, some murmurings were detected in the Russian team, who fessed up that the name sounded like slang for oral sex. There wasn't really any going back at this point, and it was agreed that, as the word 'sounded a bit like the slang', the problem was relatively minor.

To be honest, finding any word that does not sound like something in any one of the world's 7117 languages is nigh on impossible, and most companies will check any proposed brand name out in its top ten markets, or in the 23 languages that account for half the world's population. That's even before you try to register it, which is a whole different sea of pain. Just call an IP lawyer and set aside about a year to do it! It's too dull to write about here.

Most companies will check any proposed brand name out in its top ten markets, or in the 23 languages that account for half the world's population.

Figure out some basics before starting to think of any names at all

Ideally, you'd have done all the work on your strategy, explained in the earlier part of this book, and figured out your brand theme. However, if you've jumped right into this section because you really want to get your name sorted, you do need to understand who your customer is, what you are offering and how you are going to be different from the competition. Take a look at your competitors and list their names and logos, so you don't waste time on anything too similar. Then find a name that reflects what your customers want and what you do better than others. The Seatown pizzeria, which we are using as a fictitious example throughout the book, is aimed at families on holiday, where the ideal experience is that everyone gets a meal that makes them happy. A name such as Populare or Happis or Famiglia could be considered a good name to reflect this, rather than say, Papa John's or Seatown Pizzeria. What we actually chose can be found in the worked example in Part 4.

How do you find a name for your company or brand using logic?

There are a several circumstances where you don't have to do a lot of work to figure out what to call yourself:

1. Category. If you are lucky enough to be first in your category, just call it the generic name for your product or service – for example, British Gas, General Electric, Smallville Electric Cars… Those that come after you can figure out what they do. However, most new brands are not the first to market.

2. Founder. If you are well known in your field already, call the product after yourself. For example, designers generally become known for their work at a bigger fashion house before launching their own label – Tom Ford, Alexander McQueen, Gianni Versace. Many professional services firms do likewise, from global

Nice naming tales from history

Adidas

After the founder Adolf (nickname Adi) Dassler.

Amazon

After the river, which appealed to Jeff Bezos because it begins with A, so good for web searches, exotic and different and ten times bigger than the next river in the world, reflecting his ambition for the company.

Apple

Steve Jobs's favourite fruit. Simple and not inaccessible compared to IBM.

Coca-Cola

Coca leaves and kola nuts. They've taken out the cocaine nowadays, though.

GAP

The generation gap between adults and kids.

Google

A misspelling of the word 'googol', the number 10^{100}, or written out as 1 followed by 100 zeroes.

IKEA

From the initials of the founder, Ingvar Kamprad, and those of his home farm and village, Elmtaryd and Agunnaryd.

Microsoft

Combinaton of 'microcomputer' and 'software'.

Nike

The Greek goddess of victory, but was created seven years after the company was founded, it being first known as Blue Ribbon Sports.

Pepsi-Cola

Derived from 'dyspepsia', or indigestion, which the drink was originally believed to help.

Sony

Inspired by the Latin *sonus*, meaning sound, and 'sonny', a loan word from English that had become Japanese slang for a smart and presentable young man.

Volvo

Latin for 'I roll'.

consulting firms such as PricewaterhouseCoopers to advertising agencies such as Saatchi & Saatchi. Eventually the reputation of the firm and its values take over from the personal reputation of the founders. PricewaterhouseCoopers became PwC, although they did have a brief (and, in my view, daft) intervening period in 2002 when they decided to call themselves Monday. Many companies that grew into world-famous brands are named after their founders – Disney, McDonald's, Tiffany or Toyota to name only a very few – but they will by now have had decades of investment to make that name mean something to the customer.

3. Descriptive. If the product or service is likely to be the only one you make, you can create an explicit (or slightly more implicit) descriptive name deriving from it. For example, Deliveroo is a great name as long as it remains in the delivery business. Further examples are Airbnb, PayPal, Microsoft and Nescafé. Facebook is a descriptive name, being the directory handed out to university students to help them to get to know one another better. This is a US phenomenon but even a 'book of faces' gives a clue to the social networking offer of the brand. In 2021 Facebook launched an overarching corporate brand, Meta (from the word 'metaverse'), signalling the company's expansion into virtual and augmented reality. The rebranding coincided with increasing criticism and whistleblower revelations regarding business practices.

4. Acronyms. This might seem a bit dull, but many of the world's most successful brands are acronyms. You can base it on the work the company does, the products or the offer, or the founders. For example, IBM (International Business Machines), CVS pharmacy (Convenience Value Service), DHL (Dalsey Hillblom Lynn), BMW (Bayerische Motoren Werke), MAC (Make-up Art Cosmetics), and an even more clever contraction for 3M, originally Minnesota Mining and Manufacturing. Some of these acronyms, like the founder names, don't automatically conjure up meaning in the mind of the customer, so, again, decades of investment may be required to establish the name and the reputation of companies that choose this option. Or you might decide to reintroduce some meaning, as LG have: the initials originally stood for Lucky Goldstar but now the company says they stand for Life's Good – this makes sense, but does require some investment to make it stick. Of course, if you are starting your company from scratch, you can pick an acronym that can have meaning, an approach that I suspect ELF Cosmetics took – it stands for Eyes, Lips, Face but also implies cute magical beings.

How do you find a name for your company or brand if logic doesn't deliver any magic?

If none of these straightforward and logical options can work for you, there are other options to explore, most likely generating more fanciful and innovative solutions. That's not to say they will be more successful! They are generally generated by 'brainstorming'. This is a process where several people gather and generate ideas around a theme, building upon each other's ideas by word association, and suspending critical judgment. When all the ideas have been gathered, the business owners, brand director or naming agency extract the best options and can refine and build on these. A clear brief is needed for this slightly random process to yield answers that will have the right connotations, be differentiating and have customer appeal. So always start your idea-generating session with this clarity and keep it simple. For instance: 'We are looking for a name for an ice-cream brand that is indulgent but lower in sugar than its competitors. It's for adults and it will command a slight price premium over mass-market brands' or 'Our app enables book clubs to swap books with other book clubs once they have read them. Book club members are mostly women, over 30, with college degrees.'

Always start your idea-generating session with strategic clarity and keep it simple.

Desk research into other languages and the use of a thesaurus can also be ways of sourcing names, and the results of the search can be a thought starter for brainstorming. The following themes may help you explore in a more structured way:

1. Metaphors. Find metaphors that represent your brand theme or product characteristic. Nike – sportswear (the goddess of victory); Under Armour – sportswear (metal protective battle dress); Oracle – computer technology (fount of knowledge in classical mythology); Kayak – a travel app (a small watercraft, like a canoe).

2. Real words but ones that evoke something relevant, rather than describe the company. Brands such as Uber (the taxi-hailing and delivery app), which reflects a superlative; Innocent (the smoothie and food company), suggesting purity; Twitter (the short-form social networking service), evoking 'short bursts of inconsequential information' according to founder Jack Dorsey. I wonder if he still thinks this now post-Trump?

3. Unfamiliar foreign words. Latin is a good source of ideas, with Volvo ('I roll') being one of the most famous examples. Some others include Panera (a US chain of cafés) ('breadbasket' in Latin, but its origin myths also suggest it was named by combining 'pan', meaning bread in Spanish, and 'era', meaning the age) and Audi (a Latin translation of the German founder's surname, 'Horch', meaning 'hark' or 'listen'). Some Spanish and Italian names are very pleasing to the Anglo-Saxon ear but might be quite prosaic in the country of origin. If it is to be sold there, then that's a watch-out; if not, then it doesn't matter.

4. Invented words. Well, clearly you can have anything at all in this category! The simplest examples are where mergers create invented names, such as UK supermarket Asda arising from Asquith and Associated Dairies. Inventions also result from combining or misspelling words, for example Weetabix (wheat biscuit breakfast cereal); Skype (a telecommunications platform), which began as Sky-Peer-to-Peer; Accenture (a consultancy firm), which came from 'Accent on the future'; Diageo (global spirit and beer producer), which results from combining the Latin for day (*dies*) and the Greek root *geo* for world and reflects the company slogan 'Celebrating Life, Every Day, Everywhere'.

> We reached peak '–ify' in 2013, when 101 new companies ending with '–ify' were registered in the USA.

There is a plethora of other misspellings, such as Digg (a news aggregator), Lyft (a ridesharing company) and Reddit (social news aggregation and discussion). There are numerous irritating naming trends, such as the tendency for apps to omit the e in noun suffixes, like Flickr, Tumblr, Grindr, Blendr, Gathr, Readr, Qzzr. Regrettably, there are lots more. And the use of '–ify' – a trend begun by Spotify and Shopify. There are hundreds of them. We reached peak '–ify' in 2013, when 101 new companies ending with '–ify' were registered in the USA. There is even one called Brandify, offering location-based digital marketing solutions.

They look iffy to me, but I would say that, wouldn't I? Similar fads for the suffixes '–ly' and '–able' have spawned hundreds of imitators, for instance Bitly (which shortens URLs) and Mashable (a multi-platform entertainment company).

Names ending in o have quite a nice ring to them, such as Zalando (online fashion), Ayondo (an online financial trading platform) and Karosso (an online automotive marketplace).

Lots of lovely names have no logic to them… branding is an art as well as a science and a craft.

How do you judge a good name?

First, check who else is using it … someone, somewhere most likely will be. Google searches and web domain name registration companies will give you an idea on this one pretty quickly, and the latter will even suggest some pretty smart alternatives if your chosen domain is taken – perhaps suggesting substituting an s with a z and suchlike. You'll be pretty unlikely to find a unique name. It's fine to go ahead with it if the customer won't confuse the existing owner of the name with your business. Being in a different geographic region – one you never seek to trade in – or in a different category is usually just fine. Or, if you are a big company with deep pockets, you could buy the name from the company concerned.

I'd always apply my telephone test. If you had to call someone to say you worked at that company or were trying to get them to list the product, would you feel a complete twit saying that name out loud? If so, it's probably not the best name. And then, when you do say it out loud, does it have a nice ring to it? Olay sounds a lot nicer than Noxcema, for instance.

Second, what does it look like written down? Some words just look awkward – for example 'Awkward', although I'd most likely not recommend this as a brand name. Can most people read it and pronounce it? Does it work as a domain name? I struggle with a large advertising agency called Mediacom.com, even though they are an excellent organization, as well as with the UK media company Centaur, which has rebranded its marketing businesses Xeim. It's distinctive and stands for 'Excellence in marketing'. So far, so cool. I just don't know how to say it.

And then, does it evoke some sort or meaning regarding what the brand does, what it stands for, how it does things, or even its

> **If you had to call someone to say you worked at that company, would you feel a complete twit saying that name out loud?**

ambition? Does it have any derailing negative connotations? Don't worry too much about minor negatives; few names are perfect.

You may not need to be that clever

Last – and here I have to declare a bias – I prefer explicit names, especially for new products. This bias arises from knowing that few companies have the funds to invest to establish each and every new and fanciful name they come up with for their sub-brands. And customers and shareholders do tend to prefer names they can understand. If you have a master brand and are launching a new product in the range, I think it is best just to call it by the generic name, such as Tesco Value Range or Nike Sports Bras or Google Maps or Google Photos. Premium automotive brands tend to keep the product names simple, with the master brand and then a designator of size, such as BMW's 1 Series, 3 Series, 5 Series and 7 Series, or the S, C, E, etc, classes for Mercedes. Arguably, they have a narrower target than automotive brands such as Renault or Ford, the latter choosing to name its sub-brands – for example, Fiesta, Focus, Mondeo, Mustang, Puma and Galaxy. Many factors contribute to automotive companies' success, but my sense is that the brands that have to feed all these different sub-brands' mouths with marketing investment don't do well commercially.

Customers and shareholders do tend to prefer names they can understand.

Would a rose by any other name smell as sweet? I hate to diss the Bard, but in today's competitive, demand-led, branded era, it definitely wouldn't.

CHAPTER 12

What should your brand do and not do?

My grandmother used to say of my boyfriends ''andsome is as 'andsome does', and, like people, brands will be judged as much by what they do and don't do as by what they say. This is ever more significant in the days when reputations are built and trashed very fast on social media and in user reviews. Any organization can be called out when it is discovered to be hypocritical – for example, if it is found not to comply with its own policies.

In my experience, brand behaviours evolve naturally when you start to bring a strategy to life, and I would counsel against inventing the rules on this too early. If you do, you'll get overburdened with rules and regulations, some will prove unnecessary, and both will be the kiss of death for getting them adopted by the wider organization. As you begin to act on your strategy, you'll establish things you do that support the strategy and you'll get a feeling that these are things you should always do. At this point it's worth defining them and making them part of the brand guidelines.

Brand behaviour also covers the organizations that a brand might support, such as sponsorships and charity partnerships or preferred areas for staff volunteering. Of course, partnerships and sponsorships form a key aspect of marketing, and these do need to be aligned with the strategy for the brand. But this chapter deals with the less high-profile aspects of brand behaviour, which all underpin and build a well-rounded and authentic brand.

The sorts of things a brand should and shouldn't do are

Brand behaviours evolve naturally and I would counsel against inventing the rules on this too early.

infinitely variable, but the relevant 'P' pillars of classical marketing – as outlined below – are not a bad structure to help think it through. One could include an infinite variety of examples, so I have chosen Dove, a brand whose behaviour I helped to develop, and some others of particular interest.

Product

How you make your product, how you source your ingredients, and what your policies are towards companies in your supply chain can all form aspects of brand behaviour. Of course, some important ones may not actively reinforce the brand and should stay on their own merit. But those that build the brand should be noted and cherished by the CMO.

Beauty is a performance category in which transformation claims are the norm, and most are fake or flaky at best.

We developed a very clear product development strategy from the 'Honest Beauty' positioning for Dove. Beauty is a performance category in which transformation claims are the norm, and most are fake or flaky at best. A typical advertisement will say something like this: 'New Essential Face Cream from L'Elective Laboratoires with Retinol. Reduces the appearance of fine lines

The honest claims of Dove body lotion (left) compared to the pseudo-scientific and emotive copy on that of a (fictitious) competitor (right).

and wrinkles.' Most sensible people would take this to mean that your face will have fewer fine lines and wrinkles because of the retinol in this cream. But this is not what these two sentences actually say. What is true is that the product will contain retinol. But because it is separated from the next sentence by a full stop, the retinol is not the thing that is delivering the benefit. There is a name for ingredients that are there for show: 'emotive ingredients.' What this means is that they persuade the customer emotionally, but don't actually do anything.

We believed that our promise of Honest Beauty had to go deeper than the advertisements and so we set about modifying the way the products were created and marketed. We decided that we would not use emotive ingredients and would instead focus our energies on making highly efficacious products overall, mostly thanks to superior moisturization.

Point of sale
Your policy on the types of stores where you will and won't be distributed is an aspect of brand behaviour; it is easy to see that being in Nordstrom will give a different impression from being in Walmart. A brand with ethical credentials might wish to be sold only in retailers that align with these values – Whole Foods, for instance.

I think Apple's sophistication in managing the supply of iPhones to build its brand is fascinating. They are famously secretive about everything they do, so what follows is my conjecture based on my impressions of them gleaned from the way they worked with us at Vodafone.

I have a sense of Apple products as owning 'irresistible allure'. They make exquisitely beautiful products and, like people who know they are gorgeous, tend to adopt a 'come and get me' body language. This they deliver by fabulous photography and the avoidance of any sense of hard sell. They reinforce the sense of specialness by implying unattainability by restricting the supply of the phones at launch to only their own stores and their retail partners. The queues outside stores get into the press and on social media. If they didn't think this served them well, they would surely just extend opening hours.

Packaging

What you do and don't do regarding your packaging is also part of brand behaviour. The most obvious aspect of this is sustainability. However, the prospects for eco-credentials to provide differentiated positioning for a brand (or even the smaller underpinnings of brand behaviour) is eroding because everyone is trying to do it. Google returns 99 million results for a search on 'sustainable supply chains', which tells you how commonplace this activity is. Great for the planet, not so much for brand differentiation. Packaging can help to build brands in other ways. For example, a belief in the quality of your ingredients might result in your deciding that you will always have a transparent window so customers can see what they are buying. If 'unboxing' is a thing in your category, you might choose to always have packaging that is a delight to unwrap, as Apple do to reinforce their reputation for design and quality.

Driving desire through restricting supply (a long line outside an Apple store).

Singapore Airlines Staff reinforce the brand's Asian image.

Google returns

99

million

results for a search on 'sustainable supply chains'

People

When people are a critical part of the delivery of a brand, how they act and appear is fundamental to the reputation of the organization.

In B2B markets where purchases of high-value and important systems are involved, the sales people and the key account managers are vital. Most firms will have guidelines about how these individuals conduct themselves; many consulting firms adopt dress codes. None of this will make it into the customer offer. 'Buy our security software system, our salespeople don't wear suits!' is not likely to be a motivating go-to-market offer. Nevertheless, what your people wear will give an impression of the brand, hopefully the right one! The big four accountancy firms have strict dress codes, with nearly half of employees surveyed (by benchmarking firm emolument.com) saying they were restricted in the colour of their work clothes. Ernst & Young is one of the stricter companies, with 17 per cent of employees saying they were not even free to choose the colour of their socks. This sort of thing always makes headlines, but more importantly, EY has a very strong code of conduct that staff must follow, part of its ethical framework that 'underpins all that we do'. There are five categories, including how to work with other EY staff as well as concerning clients and protection of data. This is reputation-driving behaviour, and is therefore all about building the brand.

Disney promotes itself as 'the magic kingdom' and has often been in the press when its uniform rules are seen to be too draconian. Breaking the magic for this brand really matters. If a child were to see Pluto having a sneaky cigarette behind one of the theme park rides, the magic of that child's experience would be destroyed forever. I can quite understand that Disney forbids its staff from 'breaking character', and instructs them to always wear princess shoes rather than their own trainers. The French staff at Disneyland Paris rebelled about underwear rules when the park first opened. Whether a child's experience would have been compromised by seeing Pluto or Snow White wearing the wrong kind of undies is moot – one can only hope the situation did not arise.

Airlines also have strict codes of conduct and attire: Singapore Airlines (SIA) underpins its brand most overtly in this way. The famous 'Singapore Girl' wears the distinctively designed sarong kebaya and her style and character reinforce notions of Asian values and hospitality, as well as evoking caring, warm, elegant and serene attributes. This aspect of SIA's branding is not without its controversy, but as the *Straits Times* said, 'to remove the Singapore Girl icon from SIA is like removing Mickey Mouse from Disneyland'.

It's not always plain sailing, though, as the tribulations of

If a child were to see Pluto having a sneaky cigarette behind one of the theme park rides, the magic of that child's experience would be destroyed forever.

Abercrombie & Fitch will testify. For some years, this clothing retailer had a policy of employing sales staff based on physical attractiveness. Former CEO Mike Jeffries said, 'We hire good-looking people in our stores. Because good-looking people attract other good-looking people, and we want to market to cool, good-looking people.' The workers were even called models rather than sales assistants, and policies on their appearance and a strict look policy was enforced. It was reported that staff could be fired for wearing a nail decal, and, more seriously, religious clothing was banned. Several lawsuits later, in 2015, the brand declared that the 'models' would be renamed 'brand representatives' and 'body type or physical attractiveness' would no longer be a hiring criterion. The new policy would be for 'nice, smart, optimistic people'.

Tribunals rightly called the company out on this discriminatory behaviour. They were ordered to pay $40 million to ethnic minority groups, to women who were not employed in certain store positions, to a teenager with a prosthetic limb who was forced to work in a storeroom and to a Muslim woman who was ordered to remove her headscarf.

However, as long as a company remains fair to its staff and within the law, I think it should have the right to ask its staff to behave in a way that reinforces the brand. Hopefully, Abercrombie & Fitch are now getting this balance right. I'm with them on avoiding the nail decals for a clean-cut, all-American brand.

Promotion

A good example of this is Dove's advertising campaign 'Campaign for Real Beauty', which almost immediately became known as the 'Real Women' campaign in the press and among consumers. When we were creating the ads, we had to decide what we did or didn't do with regard to the casting and the photography to ensure that the integrity of the idea remained.

With regard to casting, we had to define what we meant by a real woman – after all, even Cindy Crawford is real! In the end we decided that any woman who had not had an agent at the time of casting defined her as 'real'. There was a lot of debate about whether that ruled out musicians or dancers, but we settled on the lack of agency representation as the best way we could be objective when we made those decisions. We felt that people who were paid to perform would probably not show up as authentically as women who were not. A fine distinction, but we had to make it somehow, and make it clear to 400 marketers worldwide who had to deliver their own versions of the advertising.

At the time we were creating the campaign, Kate Winslet had just had a major row with *GQ* magazine, which had stretched her cover photo image to lengthen her legs and make her look slimmer. This kind of practice, widespread in the industry, represents unrealistic ideals that affect the self-esteem of women and was one of the forces we were battling against. We had to have standards of behaviour that measured up to our ideology and we decided not to retouch or manipulate our photographs.

Our brand behaviour in this instance was not what we messaged overtly in our ads, but is an example of what we did and didn't do to uphold the integrity of our brand promise of Honest Beauty. Our customers could tell that our women were not fake, and that helped massively with their love for and trust in the brand.

As promotion becomes more and more digitally enabled, companies need to adopt policies regarding automated customer contact that work for driving sales as well as building, or at least not detracting from, the brand. For example, some simple principles on how often you email, whether and how often you serve ads on social media following searches, or what you do with abandoned online shopping baskets. Balancing the frequency and personalization of messaging with relevance, the need to avoid a sense of intrusion, or the use of customer data is a minefield that many organizations are navigating. There are whole books on this topic, so all I would say is that it is the role of the brand director to consider how this will affect the brand. Much as I love Net-a-Porter (an online retailer of designer goods) and am a regular customer, I feel they cheapen their brand by emailing me every day. I am less bothered by their discount stablemate, The Outnet, doing so. Interestingly, Apple, the master of unattainable allure, do so once a week, and, knowing them, this will not be an accident. Airbnb ensure that contacting customers about abandoned baskets does not feel like stalking and high-pressure selling, by sending highly relevant and timely messages about the destination rather than about the customer's buying behaviour. Someone who has searched

Our customers could tell that our women were not fake, and that helped massively with their love for and trust in the brand.

for a destination and when they plan to travel would be sent a prompt email giving them information regarding how far ahead other travellers to that destination typically book. And they are smart enough to send it just ahead of that typical advance booking interval.

Purpose

Whether a brand has purpose embedded at its heart or not, most organizations have some form of corporate social responsibility agenda, and cause-related marketing is increasingly popular.

When we landed on the strategy for Dove, we had to review and reboot all our charity affiliations country by country. We decided to align Dove with charities that supported women's self-esteem, such as Beat, an eating disorders association, in the UK, and in the USA a programme called Uniquely Me run by the Girl Scouts organization. Support for other charities, such as Breast Cancer, was gently and regretfully phased out. Aligning to the brand strategy involves tough calls, like following any strategy.

So, what brand behaviour might underpin our Seatown pizzeria? We could allow any customization of the pizza, unless it couldn't fit in the oven or was obscene, and kids could use a tablet to customize and order their pizza. And to keep the parents feeling secure and relaxed, we'd have wholesome ingredients, be on top of allergy issues, and offer adults in the party a large glass of wine as soon as they arrived. All noticeable aspects to underpin our families- with-kids-oriented brand.

Aligning to the brand strategy involves tough calls.

There is a lot to think about on this aspect of brand building. It does fall out naturally as you start to execute your brand strategy, but it is worth doing at the right time. Create simple guidelines and inspire your people to adopt them. I love the way that Disney told their park cleaners that a mess detracted from creating magic for their visitors. Police and punish could have been their approach, but inspiration was so much more effective.

CHAPTER 13

What should your brand look like?

An individual in a developed economy will encounter between 4,000 and 10,000 commercial messages a day and a typical supermarket carries 25,000 to 40,000 different product lines. In one research study I recall, we put cameras on the heads of shoppers and estimated how many marketing messages a shopper actually reads during their typical weekly shop and came up with just seven to eight. What a superhuman editing function humans have! And healthy self-preservation instincts.

Humans are clearly geniuses at screening out unwanted information. We can navigate the wall of spam (digital but also tinned pork) that shopping demands and choose what to buy or click on at warp speed. But it does create a challenge for brands, to stand out and to be selected at that pace. The mind uses visual shorthand, or heuristics, to make the process of choosing easier, and what your brand looks like is the most important thing you will ever decide. It's not only the logo, which is of course important, but what colours and symbols you use and how they can help or hinder your brand's success.

The study of symbols is called semiotics. There are many brand semiotic consultants who make a very good living helping companies figure this out, although their services are a bit of a luxury for most organizations. Identifying your visual assets or equities, understanding which ones the customer recognizes and loves, and then using them strongly and consistently will pay dividends for your brand.

A typical supermarket carries 25,000 to 40,000 different product lines.

Colour

Way more important than most brand managers realize, colour is probably the most crucial asset a brand can own. I once heard the CEO of Beiersdorf say that the Nivea strategy was 'blue'. I scoffed at the time, but as I matured as a marketer, I realized how much colour matters in getting customers to choose your brand.

Some brands have even trademarked their colour. Most women's hearts would beat a little faster if their partner presented them with a turquoise box tied with a white ribbon. 'Tiffany Blue' was first selected by Charles Lewis Tiffany, the company's founder, in 1845, but the colour was trademarked only in 1998. It is a custom colour also known as '1837 Blue', named for the year Tiffany & Co was started. Other trademarked colours for famous brands include 'Cadbury Purple', T-Mobile's shade of magenta, UPS's 'Pullman Brown', 'Barbie Pink', Veuve Clicquot's shade of orange, 'Culte Chinese Red' for the soles of Louboutin's shoes, and 3M's Canary Yellow for Post-it notes. Less glamorous brands also have trademarked colours, such as Owens Corning's pink loft insulation. In general, you cannot trademark the colour universally but only in the context in which it is used – on the sole of a shoe for example – or in one category, such as soft drinks. Colours in this sense are ownable brand assets and fiercely protected by the brand owners.

Lawsuits have raged for years over the protection of brands' colours. Cadbury and Nestlé were in court for 24 years over the right to use purple on products beyond just tablets of chocolate. Cadbury lost on appeal the right to change its 1995 trademark to protect the colour on its broader range. Christian Louboutin has recently won a case in the European Court of Justice stating that the red colour it applies to the sole of women's high-heeled shoes is a 'position mark'. And these are just two of dozens of legal battles involving famous brands.

Colour combinations can also be ownable and distinctive. The McDonald's red and yellow of the arches and logo is repeated wherever its brand comes to life – in stores, on packaging and in Ronald McDonald's overalls and boots. IKEA's blue and yellow is another example.

Apart from the noble aim of keeping intellectual property lawyers in cashmere coats, why do brands care?

It's pretty simple: having a distinctive colour helps customers

Brands with trademarked colours, clockwise from top left: Cat, Christian Louboutin, Cadbury, UPS, Veuve Clicquot, Coca-Cola, John Deere and Post-it.

'Tiffany Blue' was first selected by Charles Lewis Tiffany in

1845

but the colour was trademarked only in

1998

choose. And that, if you recall, is the main point of a brand. And for recognizing which brands you want at the speed of the average shopping expedition, whether in a grocery store or online, colour is a great shorthand for the customer. If you are the only red brand on a shelf of blue ones, that gives you an advantage.

Individuals typically have 70 to 100 apps installed on their smartphones, depending on where they live in the world, and use between 30 and 40 of them. Just like a grocery brand on a supermarket shelf, a brand whose app icon is a distinctive colour will be faster and easier to find. How considered the choice is will vary by category. For example, which game you fancy might be a spontaneous choice, whereas which airline you need might be more considered. So the ease of spotting an app in the more spontaneous categories, such as gaming or social media, will be crucial in driving revenue for those organizations. Many apps are advertising-funded, so the number of engagements is a fundamental commercial driver.

60% of global retail logos are red

On my own phone, with 121 apps installed, 33 are predominantly blue in colour, more than double the number of the next most popular single colour, green, at 15. This is consistent with most studies, which find that around 30 per cent of the logos in the world are blue. Blue is a colour people associate with competence, intelligence, trust, efficiency, duty and logic, so it's easy to see why many companies choose it if these values are relevant… but it doesn't provide much in the way of differentiation within a category. Financial institutions have a particular love of blue – almost half of the breakout finance apps of 2018 had blue icons. I guess you tend to have only one banking app on your phone – it's finding it among all the other blue icons that is the irritant. And why would you want customers to begin their interaction with your brand in a slightly less than positive frame of mind?

Individuals typically have 70 to 100 apps installed on their smartphones and use between 30 and 40 of them.

Retail apps, where customers might well switch quickly and whimsically between apps, seem to be a sea of red, pink and orange. In fact, 60 per cent of global retail logos are red. Red at retail often symbolizes value (you've probably noticed that Sale announcements are almost always red) as well as stimulation and excitement – which is probably why they all go down the same path. All the breakout retail apps in China in 2018 were red, apart from one, Xianyu, which is yellow.

Gaming app icons are generally characterized by an image

or a character featured in the game rather than by having one distinctive colour. I find them pretty undifferentiated, apart from a few standout examples – such as Brawl Stars, with its strong yellow skull icon, a game that was in the top five for consumer spend in five out of 12 global economies in 2018. Of course, its success might be also that it is great fun – as well as easy to find!

Logos

Frankly, you could write a whole book about logos, and many people have. The logo is a major part of a company's identity, and the more consistent and distinctive it is, the easier customers' choice will be. Perhaps the most famous logo on the planet is that of Coca-Cola, named by the company founder's bookkeeper, Frank Robinson, who thought the two Cs would look well in advertising. And he then designed the scripted look that was characteristic of penmanship at that time. It was trademarked as a logo in 1893. Apart from a somewhat aberrant redesign for a year in 1890, when it went all Art Nouveau, all Coca-Cola logos have retained the script form. Over the years it has been refreshed and evolved, but has always retained its fundamental character. Diet Coke retains the script in the word 'diet', thereby keeping faith with its parent brand. In the 1940s, the logo became inextricably linked with a characteristic red colour, which is trademarked for soft drinks by Coca-Cola.

Perhaps the most famous logo on the planet is that of Coca-Cola, named by the company founder's bookkeeper, Frank Robinson.

Coca Cola has brilliantly managed its logo's consistency for 130 years, except when it went a bit off-piste for just one of them.

1887–1890s

1890–1891

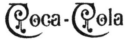

Introduced in 1941, this logotype is still used today

1958

1969

Contemporary iteration from 2016

TASTE THE FEELING

I think the best example of taking a core brand colour and extending it across many product offerings is that of Google, an art it has mastered particularly well in the age of the app. Google began life with a multicoloured logo, but it moved to the simple four primary colour version after a year, in 1998. In classical serif faces, including Baskerville Bold and Catull, it always retained the four primary colours, but switched the first letter from green to blue pretty quickly. The big shift came in 2015, when it presented a bolder, sans serif face with a unique font and a revised multicoloured G to use in icons. It has been so consistent with the four primary colours over the years, and used them in all its app icons, that you can guess which is a Google app even if you have never used it. It also keeps them simple, fresh and consistent, with regular updates, such as the recent shift in the logo of Google Maps. It is an outstanding example of visual equity management for a brand.

Like everything a brand does, the logo should communicate something about the brand. Google has always prided itself on being simple to use. And the use of straightforward, easy-to-read typefaces and primary colours reflects that. Microsoft's updated design for its Office suite of products is also outstanding, with a strong and cohesive visual style incorporating a clear indication of the functionality in each (see opposite). Premium brands tend to have logos that are dignified and somewhat recessive, rather than dominating. The Disney logo is suggestive of playfulness and magic. UPS, with its deep brown and gold and its shield, suggests dependability. SAP, with modern, chunky type on a diagonal blue background, suggests a forward-looking enterprise with a fresh outlook. Deciding on your logo is probably one of the most business-critical things an organization will do. It needs to be built to last and suggest what the brand expects to stand for for years, decades or, if you're any good at it, centuries.

Logos often are simply the company name, but many also have a symbol associated with them, and if this symbol is recognizable and ownable as well, this can help massively in the age of smartphone apps and Google searches. Where you can 'symbolize' the name, you have an easier job – consider for example the target for Target, the shell for Shell, the apple for Apple, and perhaps the most recognizable icon in many parts of the world, the red cross for the Red Cross.

Other brands may not be so lucky, but by assiduously using a simple symbol and sticking with it, some symbols have become almost as famous as the brand name itself: the swoosh for Nike, the golden arches for McDonald's, the interlocking Cs for Chanel, the rearing horse for Ferrari, the red coin logo for the Bank of China, the bird for Twitter.

Brands that originated in the age of the smartphone tend to design their logos in the mobile icon form, whereas older brands have to adapt or crush their logos into that round-cornered square. Here is where owning a distinctive colour and brand symbol or icon can be immensely useful. And those brands that don't have a readymade one are making their existing icons more prominent, such as the evolution of the owl for Tripadvisor. British Airways is another good example, with its distinctive ribbon. EasyJet perhaps had a slightly easier time of it in the aviation industry with its distinctive orange colour – you can't miss that app when booking flights on your phone! Airbnb was conceived in the smartphone era and came of age when the majority of its customers would have owned one. Its logo has a highly distinctive symbol, known internally as the Bélo, a looping symbol representing people, place, heart and the A of Airbnb. I like it as a design icon, and combined with the distinctive colour pink – not many apps are pink (7 per cent on my phone) – it stands out, so maybe you'd go there first when thinking about a trip.

Microsoft's app icons boast a distinctive, cohesive and attractive design and clear functionality signals.

Typefaces

The written word is a bigger part of a brand's identity than ever before, with even toilet cleaners having websites, Twitter feeds and email marketing. A typeface is the type design and the font is the size, weight and style of that typeface. The typeface you use will have two roles: to build the character of the brand and to present it consistently across multiple channels. I find the latter aspect delivered well in general by many brands, but brands that choose type to really add character are rarer. Either way, you will need to first select a typeface that reflects the brand identity you are creating, maybe even two – one for headlines and one for copy. Sometimes a distinctive headline font adds a lot of character but is not suitable for longer lengths of type. Generally, it is good practice to pick a typeface for written communication quite different from the logo (to keep the logo distinctive and protect its intellectual property). They all come in digital as well as print forms. Some brands have a unique typeface designed specifically for them. This is quite common with big global brands: Uber have Uber Move, we had a bespoke Vodafone face, and Cisco have Cisco Sans. Interestingly, I don't think any of these are particularly distinctive. The benefit of having your own typeface in a huge organization has more to do with maintaining consistency with a very high number of people involved in creating communications. It's a pretty unambiguous instruction to staff to use Vodafone regular. Other brands use off-the-shelf solutions. These can be purchased from a library such as FontShop or Typekit, although the licence fees for multiple users can soon add up and may exceed the cost of a bespoke face. Many start-ups choose open-source (free) options such as Google Fonts, Font Squirrel or Fontface Ninja, and the variety you can get there is sufficient to create a distinctive and appropriate look for your brand. The impression given by different typefaces is enormous, as the following images show.

Start by choosing your headline typeface. In addition to figuring out if it represents your brand well, you also need to consider if it complements your logo, its legibility in the forms and sizes it will be used, whether there are sufficient forms to work in print and digital, and is it future-proofed with a big enough variety and weight of forms? It's probably a good idea to select two or three at first because you then need to match it

Typefaces add character to the brand.

The typeface you use will have two roles: to build the character of the brand and to present it consistently across multiple channels.

Duo's wing inspired ascender
short ascenders
flicked 'g' inspired by Duo's eyes
circular low-contrast
wing tipped stem junction
wide letter proportions

Duo

Feather bold

go further
go faster
go anywhere

Language never stands still.

Nor do we.

Feather bold

abcdefghijklmn
opqrstuvwxyz
ABCDEFGHIJKLMN
OPQRSTUVWXYZ
àáâãäāăå
0123456789

 Goodbye language barriers.

as easy as uno dos tres

astonishing science. spectacular museum.

SCIE
NCE
MUS
EUM

SM GRID

ABCDEFG

EiEMW

abdefg

01234

OUTLINE

with a body copy font, so a couple of options to play around with can help get it right. Fortunately, there are digital tools to help with that, such as Font Pair and Flipping Typical. Once you've decided, you need to map out where they will typically be used as a guide for people to follow. Try to keep this simple, and don't legislate for everything. Classifications such as headlines, subheads, body copy and packaging should be sufficient. The typeface is usually a big part of a brand's guidelines. Duo Lingo and the Science Museum are two examples where the typeface adds character to the brand and has all the necessary flexibility.

Typefaces make a big difference to the overall impression.

Brand icons or mascots

Brands often have a distinctive character associated with them, and these are hugely valuable to that company in driving recognition and likeability. Milka, whose strategic evolution I led and described in Chapter 10, is loved by families all over Eastern and Western Europe. It has a much-loved icon, a lilac and white cow called Lila. People pay good money for pencil cases, rucksacks and other items representing her. When I joined Mondelez, I could not understand why she was not front and centre of the advertising… and when we refreshed the pan-regional campaign, that is exactly where we put her. We made Lila the heroine of our TV commercials, and sales went up in every country where they ran. Cadbury Dairy Milk's glass and a half of milk is another example of a brand icon that was developed further when I was leading the brand at Mondelez. We gave it more emphasis by modernizing its design, making it more prominent and inextricably linking it to the logo.

Another success story that leveraged a brand icon was work done on the Guinness can by the design agency Jones Knowles

Ritchie. They have a 'less is more' approach to packaging design, a view that I heartily endorse, and they did some research where they asked Guinness drinkers to draw the brand. Time after time, customers drew the harp symbol. The black and white colour of the drink itself or the Guinness logo had been considered the most important assets until this point. The agency simplified the can, made the harp the most prominent feature and made it golden. Not only was the can beautiful, it stood out so much better because it was uncomplicated and was instantly recognizable to the shopper. The transformation is shown on page 185.

Brands have been using icons for more than 100 years. The Michelin Man, reputed to be the world's oldest brand mascot, was born in 1894; the Pillsbury Doughboy, officially named Poppin' Fresh, first appeared in 1965 and made a memorable appearance in giant form in the movie *Ghostbusters* nearly 20 years later. Colonel Sanders for KFC, Tony the Tiger for Kellogg's Frosties, the Duracell bunny – the list goes on and on.

Bibendum the Michelin Man, reputed to be the world's oldest brand mascot, was born in 1894.

Perhaps most familiar from the supermarket aisle, such mascots are plentiful in tech or digital brands as well, although less so in more traditional B2B brands. The little green robot symbol for the Android operating system and the windows for Microsoft Windows (a tad literal, but they are a somewhat right-brained organization!) are familiar to most. At the B2B end of the tech spectrum are the owl for Hootsuite, Freddie the chimp for MailChimp, and Duke the red-nosed penguin for Oracle's Java.

Design style

Wherever the brand shows up, on websites, in stores and in advertising, it should have a signature look that expresses its identity. And it should consistently use a limited selection of colours and visual styles that reflect that.

Premium brands often provide the best examples of design style for brands, as their benefits are often intangible, rather than a 'washes whiter' type of performance claim. 'Makes you look richer' is not something you would want to be overt about, even though that is what you might want to communicate! Not in most countries anyhow.

One very good example of this is Calvin Klein. The brand's sensual and provocative style, using young models and partial nudity, caused particular uproar in 1980 when it used the 15-year-old Brooke Shields claiming to wear nothing under her CK jeans. In the early 1990s it began to adopt black-and-white photography, with a style dubbed 'heroin chic' thanks to its featuring young and very slim models such as Kate Moss. Whether you approve or not, it's undeniable that its style did much to create the brand, from fragrances such as Obsession and CK One to its ranges of underwear.

Monochrome seems to be a characteristic of many premium brands: BMW, Mercedes and Audi car showrooms are universally grey, white and silver. And Apple tend to be a past-master at understated allure, although in 2013 they went off-piste, in my view, when they launched their very different 5c iPhone range with its plastic casing in bright colours, a step that many feel was not their finest hour commercially. Apple are notoriously private about their commercial data, but you may draw your own conclusions from the fact that this approach was not repeated.

I think it is an example of an organization going radically 'off-brand' – a step that generally leads to lack of success in my experience.

Some premium brands do have a more maximalist approach. A great example is the iconic London store Harrods, with an olive-green and gold colour theme (sported proudly by shoppers on their carrier bags) and a luxurious interior with much gilt and plush, including the lavish Egyptian escalator. Bling doesn't even begin to describe it. But it is classy bling! Dolce & Gabbana is another brand that distinguishes itself by expressing itself in a more extrovert celebration of *la dolce vita* with curvaceous women, rather than following the herd of understated luxury competitors with androgynous models.

More mass-market brands also build their brand by visual style. We defined 'Beautifully Uncomplicated' as a key aspect of the Dove brand and both the packaging and the advertising reflected this. With white dominating, touches of blue and an uncluttered style, it had the added advantage of making the brand look more premium and fresh compared to its rivals, whose advertising and packaging was very busy. US retailer Target have red, white and target symbols as obvious manifestations of their brand in-store. But they also inject subtler cues as well, such as circular light fittings. Retail store design is big business, and is a critical part of building those brands.

Generally, brands also have what they call a secondary palette, a selection of additional colours and materials that complement the main brand colours and whose use will deliver a consistent look to any manifestations of the brand. These come into their own especially in websites or retail premises, where the relentless use of the brand's principal colours might be monotonously overbearing. If these secondary colours were not mandated, brand consistency would break down as the design elements would soon be applied at random. A complex website often has different teams responsible for different elements of it, and if too much discretion were given to them, customers would navigate from page to page with an experience that potentially jars. The experience would be inconsistent and would make customers' feelings about it less clear.

A photographic style will also be part of building brands, especially in fashion and beauty. Nivea typically feature smiling, pretty, fresh-faced and girl-next-door type models, posed and looking directly to camera with blurred-out settings (and, of course, lots of blue!). The Dove style was more spontaneous (real women are less trained to pose!) and was best achieved, in my view, by the photographer Rankin, who would close the camera shutter just when every woman in the ad felt confident – and it showed in the final results. In every ad, our women were posed against a limbo white background. L'Oréal ads have an unequivocally glossier look and feature famous celebrities such as Eva Longoria, Celine Dion, Jane Fonda or Jennifer Lopez. These three huge global beauty brands have each created a distinctive, ownable look, with a variety of style elements contributing. Each makes a different statement about the brand. Dove: Real; Nivea: Wholesome; L'Oréal: Glamorous.

When you think about it, what a person looks like is a large part of their ability to be recognized and to have other people establish or rekindle feelings about them. If every time a person met you, you looked quite different, they might not even know it was you at all, and certainly would not know what to make of you in the end. And brands are no different. Visual identity is arguably the most powerful aspect of a brand and needs careful thought and tight control.

Visual identity is arguably the most powerful aspect of a brand and needs careful thought and tight control.

Managing the creativity of an organization and keeping the brand's visual face to customers consistent is a never-ending balancing act. I favour some very clear and straightforward 'must obey' rules with a relatively small number of individuals empowered to decide. Then let some creativity flow. But this freedom has to be tempered with regular reviews of the good, the bad and the ugly executions, with the potential to revoke the licence to operate. That must go hand in hand with celebration for examples of great innovation consistent with the brand guidelines. A 'steal with pride' culture rather than a 'not invented here' culture underpins this and should be encouraged. This is often called 'freedom within a framework' – an approach that I've found works pretty well despite a name that sounds as though it had its origins in the sitcom *The Office*.

CHAPTER 14

What should your brand's tone and manner be?

Tone and manner – sometimes called 'voice' – are elements of a brand's nonverbal communication. Psychologist Albert Mehrabian identified nonverbal elements in human interactions as contributing 93 per cent of the total communication of the message. Of this, tone and manner contributed 38 per cent. How your brand communicates is as important as what it says. And this is even more true now in such a multi-channel world, where conventions in each channel can differ and so many different individuals in a company have to deliver so many brand messages every day. Tweets and emails are missives that often go to customers daily, building a sense of the brand every time and over many different messages, from service updates to marketing promotions. The tone and manner are often the only thing that holds communication together for the brand on channels such as Twitter. And Twitter's character limit has created a whole new language incorporating hashtags, emojis and abbreviations such as TIL ('today I learned') and ICMI ('in case you missed it') for brands to adopt and play with (or not).

Tone of voice is an important executional lever for your brand, and you will need to describe one that supports the brand theme and the right to win and plays to the customer insight. If it does all these, it will express the personality of your brand and build it brilliantly.

Consider the difference between these headlines for a toilet cleaner: 'Kills all known germs' and 'Kills all known germs.

> **Tone and manner are often the only thing that holds communication together for the brand on channels such as Twitter.**

Dead.' Same message but evoking a different feeling. It's the tone
rather than the message itself that makes that cleaner feel like
a powerful killer. I want that one down my toilet! If you walked
into Fortnum & Mason in London, arguably the poshest
department store in the UK, and an assistant greeted you with
'Hi there!' rather than 'Good morning, Sir', your impression of
the brand as one that supplies groceries to the Queen of
England would be let down a little bit. Consider the difference
between tweets for new products for Fenty Beauty and Estée
Lauder shown below. Both include the Twitter convention of
using emojis, but they are building very distinct brands. Fenty
asks who 'copped' their new product while Estée Lauder's
customers attend soirées!

It's worth adding that other languages often struggle to
replicate a particular tone when translated from English. This
is partly because English generally contains more words than
other languages – some estimates put the English vocabulary
at double that of Spanish, for example. The reason is its dual
Germanic and Latin roots, meaning that English has two words
for almost everything. This is even more significant when
translating into pictographic languages such as Chinese, where
translators typically focus on sense rather than style. You will
need to communicate both sense and style to the writers. And
I'd always get an independent back-translation for important
communication assets. Missteps are much more common than

Estée Lauder ✓ @EsteeLauder . Jan 16, 2019
43.6k Tweets   Follow

Whether you're jetsetting ✈ or turning heads at an evening ✈
soiree, NEW #DoubleWear Stay-in-Place Matte Powder Foundation
is ready for any moment in your day. Find your perfect match now:
estee.com/2RwF5Ir#DoubleWearOrNothing

Fenty and Estée Lauder
have very different brand
tones.

FENTY BEAUTY ✓ @fentybeauty . Jan 12, 2019
43.6k Tweets   Follow

Roll call!! Who copped that new FENTY BEAUTY today
and what'd y'all get??

you might think. So it's best not to rely on pure translation to deliver a tone of voice if you are managing a global brand, but rather to identify a clear description of the tone you are aiming for and then let local writers figure out how to deliver both sense and style in the local language. In branding and marketing, this is known as transliteration.

Chapter 15 explores how auditory identity is increasingly important for branding as people's connection with brands is through their devices. But tone of voice applies more to the written word and voiceovers: setting a clear direction on how you speak or write makes the choice of copy style and voiceover artists easier.

The tone and manner of your brand are, of course, also delivered by the staff that your customers meet. Call centre staff are often drilled in what to say and what not to say to customers and automation is used in chat functions until a real person is needed to interact with the customer. Keeping that transition seamless creates a more cohesive brand experience. But channel conventions do vary, chat functions being accepted by customers as more informal than email, for instance.

I think some tone of voice guides go too far in telling staff exactly what to say, which can make them awkward with customers. I prefer to pick three or four approaches and then underpin this by including in training or inductions why these approaches will be relevant to the customer and appropriate for the brand. It's what I began to do at Vodafone; and the luxury hotel chain Ritz-Carlton, for example, is a master at this.

At Vodafone, our strategy could be summarized as follows: 'Our customers depend on us to live, to love and to work. As a brand of substance, the strength of our network supports their bolder lives.' As a way to enhance our understanding of dependent customers, we used the metaphor of caring for individuals with paraplegia. And I explored how someone with a severe physical impairment might prefer to be treated, so as to formulate the best tone of voice. I selected three guiding principles. Capable: for example, they would want you to get things right, to arrive on time, to give them any medications accurately and to lift them properly. We would bring out and emphasize our capability in our communication, stressing action, effort, results, deliverables. And of course, we'd make sure we did what we said we would do. Empathetic: the dictionary definition of this is being able to identify with the feelings, thoughts and attitudes of others. I also felt strongly that it was important not to patronize or talk down to any individual, especially those who might be vulnerable. Empathy felt eye-level, whereas the alternative I considered, sympathy, did not. We would listen, we would understand, we would apologize if things were our fault. Mobile phone networks and contracts are complex, and are full of jargon. Clear: being confusing to someone vulnerable or dependent would be distressing for them. So it was important that our communication was clear. We settled on three approaches to how we communicated with our customers: 'Capable, Empathetic and Clear.' Easy for customer-facing colleagues to remember, relevant for customers and appropriate for a brand of strength and substance.

We were unfortunate enough to experience a network outage when the strategy was in its early stages of adoption. Ten per cent of the network went down, a matter significant enough to get us in the national press. As a matter of protocol, at the time a crisis erupted the most fitting director on site at HQ was put in charge, and in this instance this was our chief legal counsel. I had already shared the draft brand strategy with her, including how it would impact our tone of voice in comms. Of course, the main focus was getting the network back up and running, but customer communications were very important and there was no time to check in with anyone else. Actually, even if she had wanted to check with me, she couldn't because I was in a part of the country where the network wasn't working! The following message was sent to customers: 'Some of our customers have been experiencing problems with our network. We are really sorry, and we have engineers working round the clock to fix it. We will give you an update at midday.' I think this is a perfect example of being Capable, Empathetic and Clear. And I understand that this was the first time Vodafone had ever apologized to its customers. How did it build the brand? Well, it resulted in much less reputational damage than might have occurred, with the press headline being: 'Vodafone engineers working round the clock to fix problem.'

With Dove, we had noticed how patronizing the beauty ads from some other brands were, and as a result, our brand

Our brand guidelines stated that it was important to have an 'eye-level' tone with our customers.

let's face it, firming the thighs
of a size 8 supermodel is no challenge.

There's not much point in testing a new firming lotion on size-eight
supermodel thighs, is there? That's why Dove's Firming range was tested on
ordinary women with real lives to live – and real, curvy thighs to firm.
After using Dove's nourishing and effective combination of moisturisers and
seaweed extracts, we asked if they'll go in front of the camera. What better
way to show the unretouched, unairbrushed results?

new Dove Firming Range

Dove presents the latest thing to wear
with your *yes, they're real and they're fabulous* top...

...beautiful
underarms.

Dove deodorant's formula
gives you noticeably soft,
smooth underarms in just
seven days.

Effective protection. Beautiful result.

guidelines stated that it was important to have an 'eye-level'
tone with our customers. Hence the headline in the first ad we
ran for our Campaign for Real Beauty: 'Let's face it, firming the
thighs of a size 8 supermodel is no challenge' (above left) and
continued with ads such as the playful one for deodorant
(above right): 'Dove presents the latest thing to wear with your
"yes they're real and they're fabulous" top.'

Dove's tone is always
'eye-level'.

I've not found a good toolkit to figure out tone of voice; any
that exist seem to me to reduce potential more than they aid
thinking. I'd recommend just some good brains and some good
writers and a little trial and error. Just aim for very few thoughts
or words that sum up your tone of voice. Three or four. Or even
better, just the one! Just test any you select as follows. Might
another brand reasonably choose the antonym? For example, if
you chose 'irreverent', another brand might legitimately prefer
'respectful'. Or if 'enthusiastic', another brand might want to be
'laid back' or 'understated'. But if you chose 'human', it's pretty
unlikely that another brand would want to be 'robotic'. Or 'honest'
as opposed to what exactly? Devious? Disingenuous? Brand
guidelines are littered with anodyne tone of voice descriptions.

I've seen 'honest' and 'human' in far too many brand guidelines – words like this won't help a copywriter deliver your website – and watch eyes roll if you try to teach your customer-facing staff to adopt this manner. The leading global branding agency, Landor, approaches the matter of tone by choosing famous characters who talk in a particular way. For instance, they suggested Doc Brown from *Back to the Future* for a brand of software development I worked for, where we wanted to be geeky, eccentric and enthusiastic. They believe their copywriters find this easier to write to. Whatever works, I say, as long as it delivers.

I've seen 'honest' and 'human' in far too many brand guidelines – words like this won't help a copywriter deliver your website.

For our Seatown pizzeria (the slightly premium restaurant for families on holiday, where everyone can create their favourite pizza, resulting in a happy and harmonious meal) a tone of voice that would be appropriate would be 'Loving and a little bit Italian'. Imagine a nonna pinching the cheeks of a bambino who knows she loves him, so he settles down to eat without fuss, basking in her happy confidence.

Here are some other great examples of very different brands that have a particularly distinctive tone:

Mailchimp. The world-leading email marketing software company has chosen to present a quirky personality and builds on the company's values of fun, creativity and independence. Its website answers 'Why Mailchimp?' with 'Helping you build your thing is our thing' and 'Let's Get Growing'. Once signed up, the interaction continues in a clear, quirky and colloquial way. When you send out an email, it captures the sense of anxiety you feel before you send it to thousands of people with an image of the send button and a cartoon of their mascot Freddie's arm dripping with sweat. Once the mail is sent to your database, your feeing of triumph is captured with a message from Freddie, offering you a 'Hi Five!'

Tiffany, whose principal branding asset is the blue colour, has a tone of voice that is restrained, elegant and judiciously witty in channels where this is a convention. Online, you might be offered 'six ways to elevate your home' or advised that 'There's no question too small or request too big for our Tiffany customer service experts'. Ads also use a pure and plain style of language, with billboard headlines like 'Believe in love' and 'Capturing the light of dawn'. Tweets are wittier: for example one says, 'The only thing blue about Monday should be a Tiffany blue box.'

Sentence construction is full and grammatical, with no trendy vernacular or gimmicks. Some might not notice the subtlety of this, as it is so classic, but I think it cleverly reinforces Tiffany's timeless and upmarket brand. And I have no doubt that it takes quite a lot of management to maintain this tone by refusing to allow the funky and trendy that creative people often want to introduce.

Harley-Davidson capture their outlaw character perfectly in their tone of voice. On their website, they have buttons with 'Check it out' and product descriptors such as 'Agile and ready to blast through streets'. In advertising, their brand tone really booms. They choose short punchy headlines in their ads, with a manner that I would describe as emphatic, macho, rebellious, witty with a dash of shock. Written in all capital letters for added oomph, examples are 'Don't Wannabe', 'Screw it. Let's Ride', 'Beach Balls', 'Morning Donut', 'Unfollow' or 'The Meek Inherit Nothing'. They do try to attract woman riders with ads like 'Soccer Mom' and 'Fatboy Meets Girl', but were a shade less female-friendly in an ad that ran in 2005 in Germany showing a shaggy-bearded biker aged about 40, with the line: 'I wouldn't let my wife ride it. At least not 'til she's 18.'

'Doesn't Your Family Deserve Private Healthcare? Maybe. Maybe Not.' Harley-Davidson has an outlaw tone, even going so far as to suggest that owning one is 'a completely irresponsible thing to do'.

Missguided, an online clothing retailer aimed at young women, state that they are a bold, straight-talking, fashion-forward brand. Their mission is 'to empower females globally to be confident in themselves and be who they want to be'. Embracing street style and popular culture, this very much informs how they write. On their 'about' page, they say that 'Babe Power' is at the heart of the brand, and also introduce the CEO with the question 'Who run this mother?', referencing the lyrics of Beyoncé's song 'Who Run the World (Girls)'. Tweets and communications to customers are full of emojis and call customers Babe, while the hashtag #BabesOfMissguided encourages a sense of belonging among them. They describe their selection of fitted dresses as 'it's all about the bod' and their eyelashes as 'there's nothing like a good pair of falsies to perfect a night-time makeup look'; for clear high heels they urge girls to 'channel those Kardashian vibes'. Building brand loyalty by making their customers feel part of an empowered sisterhood is very much delivered by their tone of voice.

The written word is not the only way tone and manner can build brands, although it is arguably one that is easier to control. Harder to implement and maintain is how sales associates, restaurant servers or front-of-house hospitality staff address customers. But this is even more crucial.

The Ritz-Carlton regularly come top of rankings of guest satisfaction and are a very upmarket hospitality option. Their service 'motto' is 'We are ladies and gentlemen serving ladies and gentlemen', which staff are asked to apply not only to guests but also to colleagues. Staff are addressed as 'ladies and gentlemen' and are listened to regarding their experiences and ideas for improvement. Some parts of the training are prescriptive. For example, they teach staff to give guests a warm and sincere greeting, using their name, but it is the underlying ethos of dignity and respect that is more powerful. It creates a way of speaking to customers that reinforces Ritz-Carlton's brand as one with 'a warm, relaxed and refined ambience providing the finest personal service and facilities for its guests'. Is it tone or is it service? Probably both, and seamlessly integrated – hallmarks of a truly great brand.

What should your brand smell, taste, feel and sound like?

Science and common sense tell us that our five senses (sight, smell, taste, touch and hearing) are highly evocative of feelings. And a brand's reputation, being a combination of reason and emotion, is built by managing these 'sensory equities'. Chapter 13 dealt with the most universal and dominant of these in brand execution: sight. This chapter covers the remaining four.

Of course, some of these equities are obviously core to the brand: a perfume brand has to have a characteristic smell, a meal from a fast-food chain will have a characteristic taste, radio brands will have a characteristic sound and cars will feel a certain way to drive.

If the sensory equity is core to the brand, clarifying what the key elements are and enabling operational mechanisms to keep them consistent is more work than many might imagine. For others, the sensory equities are secondary, but might still have a big role in building the brand. Brands that show up in the real world will potentially have all five equities to manage, whereas digital brands will be focused on visual and auditory equities, and will have to work harder at building distinctiveness since they are playing with fewer senses.

This chapter looks at the four senses other than sight, illustrating both their core and their contributory roles in building brands.

Smell

Smell is the sense most closely associated with memory and emotions. Smell is hardwired to the limbic system of the brain, which is also responsible for decision-making and emotions. The potential to use smell to enhance customers' propensity to remember, prefer and choose a brand is obvious when you think about it. A study done at Iowa State University showed purchase intent for a brand increasing threefold when a fragrance consistent with the brand's imagery was added at the point of sale. Concordia University in Quebec did a study showing that lobbies of hotels fragranced in a way that fitted the hotel's brand image increased perceptions of comfort and cleanliness as well as propensity for customers to recommend the hotel. Because it can be so powerful, some brands develop a proprietary, signature scent, even if they are not fragrance-focused brands.

Smell is the sense most closely associated with memory and emotions.

Retaining a characteristic smell for a fragrance across formats and in product innovations is actually an art. The legendary Chanel No. 5 has a characteristic smell described as woody, powdery and floral, with notes including jasmine and rose underpinned by sensual musk, all enlivened with aldehydes. This characteristic scent has to show up in different perfume concentrations and in a variety of products, from bath soap to body lotion to hair mist. To contemporize the brand, there are now four further fragrance variants – 'sensual', 'woody', 'airy' and 'fresh' – all embodying aspects consistent with the original. For example, No. 5 L'eau, the fresh variant, is aimed at millennials and still has the jasmine, rose and musk, but also citrussy top notes. Managing all this, with complex supply chains involving variations in natural ingredients sourced from all over the world from France to Madagascar is an epic challenge. It's obvious it has to be done, but that doesn't make it easy. I imagine if I knew the details of exactly how this was accomplished, I would have to be killed.

Food retailing uses smell in a very direct way, mostly arising naturally from the lovely goods being created. Sometimes it is more deliberately and, some would say, cynically activated. For example, Cinnabon ensure that its rolls are baked every 30 minutes to attract customers all day long with their distinctive aroma. Keeping ovens close to the front door and the ventilation hoods on a weak setting is another tactic used by food brands,

Cinnabon ensure that its rolls are baked every 30 minutes to attract customers all day long with their distinctive aroma.

especially bakeries. When a brand doesn't manufacture on the premises, artificial fragrancing can be deployed. The M&M's concept store in London didn't smell as you'd expect it to, like chocolate, until aroma was added, and Hershey did a similar thing with their store in Times Square.

Fragrance can be important without being central to the brand's benefit. Nivea is about care for the skin, but its fragrance contributes significantly to your feelings about the brand. The smell of Nivea is strongly evocative, one you typically first encounter on a seaside holiday when your mum liberally smears it over your wee naked body. An advertising experiment illustrates the power of its aroma. One cinema was sprayed with Nivea's fragrance and a Nivea commercial was shown in the normal reel of ads. Another auditorium showed the same ads but was not fragranced. The recall of the Nivea commercial was 515 per cent higher in the one that had the Nivea perfume. A few years ago, I was chatting to a researcher who was testing advertising concepts for Nivea for Men and she told me that any attempt to portray sexy images in the ads provoked outrage among men in the focus groups. We both agreed that the mummy-smearing on holiday beaches was at the root of that reaction! And may explain why Nivea retains its wholesome image – and so it should.

Nivea's fragrance is consistent across its product range

Singapore Airlines uses fragrance (in this case infusing hot towels) to reinforce a sense of Asia.

Visitor attractions are, of course, brands, and fragrance can be very much part of the experience. A quirky example is the London Dungeon, which 'enlivens exhibits' with smell, choosing from a menu offered by a fragrance house, including 'vomit', 'urine' and 'decaying flesh'.

As the hotel lobby example mentioned earlier illustrates, fragrances can build brands when the nature of the smell fits well with it even if fragrance is not directly related to what the brand offers. Singapore Airlines uses its own trademarked fragrance, 'Stefan Floridian Waters', blending rose, lavender and citrus, which is worn by crew and used in hot towels and in the aircon. This reinforces the Asian origins of the brand and evokes memories of quality and service in repeat customers.

Speedo wanted the smell of the Australian coast in their concept stores, New Balance shoe shops in China incorporated notes of wood and leather to signal heritage and craftsmanship, Mercedes-Benz put their signature, citrussy in-car fragrance 'Freeside Mood' in every vehicle. The effect on customers may be conscious or unconscious, but whichever the case, done right, smell will help customers prefer and choose your brand.

Taste

Taste is almost always intrinsic to food and drink brands and is generally not a secondary brand characteristic for other categories. Tasting good is pretty much a given, but what has to be determined is what defines that characteristic taste in particular and therefore can be used consistently to build the brand. As the range extends or you move to a new category, you will need to figure out what should and shouldn't vary and how to deliver on that, given complexities of sourcing and formulations.

People are always delighted to find that their favourite fast food tastes pretty much the same from KFCs, Taco Bells and McDonald's around the world. Of course, these firms also cater to different national cuisines: McDonald's has a Teriyaki McBurger in Japan, and a Sichuan Double Chicken Burger, sweet taro pie and even congee in China. Meticulous management enforces consistent recipes and culinary practice even when crossing borders and adapting to local tastes. And that is one of the reasons these brands are trusted and reassuring. Because they are consistent.

The mighty Coca-Cola famously got into trouble on the matter of flavour when in 1985 they launched 'New Coke', which they had to abandon within three months. Research showed that when they didn't know what brand they were drinking customers actually preferred it – but they hated it when they did. Limbic systems were in overdrive. It wasn't the Coke they knew and loved, and they weren't having it.

Coca-Cola famously got into trouble on the matter of flavour when in 1985 they launched 'New Coke'.

Tastes vary hugely across cultures and even the exact same product can vary to cater for different national taste preferences. Heinz Tomato Ketchup has one basic recipe but local variants – sweeter versions for the Canadians, Brits, Australians and Venezuelans and spicier for the USA and mainland Europe. Sometimes global differences are unexpected because they don't seem to be dependent on food culture: one example of this is chocolate. At Mondelez we knew that whatever brand of chocolate customers were given as a child acculturates their taste for a particular chocolate taste for life. British chocolate lovers, reared on Cadbury, think Hershey's chocolate tastes like sick, and some Americans don't much like Cadbury either. Europeans prefer another Mondelez brand they grew up with, the sweet, creamy Milka, with its famous 'tender' texture.

At Cadbury, we discovered that customers did not prefer Cadbury Dairy Milk to its nearest rival in unbranded taste tests and so a recipe improvement project began. The team had to maintain the characteristic taste, and the basic recipe stayed the same, but they found that finer-milled cocoa and rounding the shape of the square did the trick for customer preference. One reason chocolate is so delicious is because it melts just below blood temperature. The rounder shape of squares fitted the roof of the mouth better and made the experience of eating it much nicer thanks to the way it melted more easily. Also, the finer milling of the cocoa made the chocolate feel smoother. This sort of thing is called 'organoleptics' or 'mouthfeel' – both rather inelegant terms for the rather wonderful art of making food more delicious! And arguably as much about touch as taste.

As brands expand away from their core product, they need to decide on the characteristic taste that defines the brand and which will appear everywhere. Nando's Peri-Peri chicken made its way to their range of sauces and then to the mayonnaises, all with its characteristic chilli flavour. Bombay Sapphire gin retains its characteristic floral botanical notes across its variants. Toblerone always has honey and almond nougat.

Feel

According to psychologists, touching something creates a sense of ownership and is therefore an element that contributes significantly to purchase intent, which is of course part of the point of a brand. Also known as haptic marketing, how your brand feels is critical, especially in creating perceptions of quality. And like other aspects of sensory branding, it can be either central to the brand or a more supporting aspect.

The feel of a car is intrinsic to the brand offer. Automotive brands will invest millions in ensuring that the feel of the brand is congruent with the overall proposition. The ride quality, handling, how tight the steering is, door-closing mechanics and the texture and touch of the leather interiors will all receive major investments of time and millions of dollars. A Mercedes S Class and a Porsche feel very different to drive. Volkswagen even made a TV commercial about the obsession of its engineers with the door closure. The feel of beauty products and their packaging is absolutely vital, especially in premium cosmetics. Even in the mass market, Dove's core equity, 'one quarter moisturizing cream', meant that every product had to have a creamy texture, and TV commercials performed less well if we omitted the creamy 'pour shot'.

Volkswagen even made a TV commercial about the obsession of its engineers with the door closure.

How a food feels to eat (organoleptics or mouthfeel) is almost as important as taste. For Milka, being a 'tender chocolate' – soft-textured, creamy and melty – was the main product benefit of that brand.

Many brands still take great care of this aspect even if it's not an overt part of their strategy, mostly to create quality perceptions. The quality of paper stock has always been critical for newspaper and magazine brands, although the nature of their content would be front and centre of their offer. Dishwashing brands might want to be viscous to suggest efficacy, for example, and shampoos might choose a rich lather to reinforce the idea of nourishing care.

The swipe right or left is a big part of the Tinder dating app experience and haptics are big in gaming with vibrational controllers and force-feedback. Apple designs haptics into its products – for example the sense of a ratcheted wheel when setting time in the iPhone's alarm function, or when you click on a Mac's trackpad. It's such an important aspect of the Apple brand that it has open-source haptic guidelines for app developers.

In some categories, touch is such a critical part of purchase behaviour that customers are very unlikely to buy the product unless they have felt it. Even with e-commerce dominating our lives, this is still true. If that dress doesn't feel as silky as it looked online, it will be going straight back, with the added sting of customer disappointment.

Sound

Sonic branding has been around for more than a century, pretty much since the advent of radio, but the arrival of mobile devices and now digital assistants has transformed the possibilities. Many more brands are now figuring out how to build their brand with sound, and a whole industry of sonic branding agencies has sprung up to help them.

Brands for which sound is core include radio stations, podcasts, record labels, bands and musicians. I happen to think that bands and musicians are brands, although some might not like the term. The listening experience defines these brands as much as a jingle or sonic logo, although all should mutually reinforce each other. Many radio stations will have a musical theme played regularly throughout the broadcasts. This 'radio imaging' includes 'sweepers', 'djdrops' 'artistdrops' or 'ramps' to pop into broadcasts as much to remind people which station they are listening to as to build the brand identity. Heart, the largest commercial radio station in the UK, has a cheerful 'This is Heart' jingle for its brand of feelgood music. LA-based Power 106, which claims to 'own Hip Hop', has an appropriate drum and siren backing their identity. The music for BBC News channels reaches 394 million global listeners and contains the iconic 'pips' that originated from the sounds used to mark the hour. However, the rapidly emerging podcast industry has been slow to use sonic branding. Serial, with its tinkly piano intro, TED Talks and the BBC do, but even for world-leading podcast series, there is very little. In my view, this is a missed opportunity. Jim Reekes, a former Apple executive, lamented the loss of the Mac's characteristic start-up chime, saying, 'It's like sitting down at a restaurant and there's no one there to greet you'. I'm with Jim on that and feel the same when starting a podcast.

Sonic branding for movie entertainment brands goes way back. For example, MGM's roaring lion has been its trademark

MGM's roaring lion has been its trademark since 1928.

Brands with strong sonic identity.

since 1928, when its first 'talkie' was launched. James Bond and *Game of Thrones* are brands, and the music associated with them is a huge generator of their emotional pull. And who cannot be thrilled by the two beat 'ta-dum' at the start of a new Netflix series? For me this is inexorably connected to my enjoyment of *House of Cards*, from which the sonic logo was allegedly derived, reflecting the table-knock performed by the series' anti-hero.

Many digital brands don't have all the senses to leverage and so rely more on sound. Famous examples include Microsoft's distinctive chords for Windows, which was composed by Brian Eno, Intel's five notes, allegedly played somewhere in the world every five minutes, and Xbox's complex blend of whooshing and 'soft hit' sounds, which raises the pulse of gamers all over the world.

Intel's five notes are allegedly played somewhere in the world every five minutes.

It is possible to trademark a sound for your brand under a World Trade Organization intellectual property rights agreement established in 1989. Harley-Davidson tried to trademark their 'potato potato potato' engine noise in 1994 but they ultimately failed because their legal team could not prove that it was truly unique and not previously produced by any other motor. Despite this, it is still a cherished feature of one of the world's most iconic brands. As electric cars are becoming common, artificial engine noise is having to be added for safety reasons, and that sound is being engineered differently by different brands to reflect their character. One day a sound chip will deliver the throaty roar of an electric Lamborghini. I feel a bit sad about that.

Many brands used advertising jingles or soundtracks to create impact, recognition and emotion. And some of these elements made it beyond the communication or marketing right to the core of the brand. The Flower Duet from Delibes's opera *Lakmé* made its debut in British Airways' celebrated 'Face' TV commercial in 1989 and has been part of the on-board experience ever since. Audi are using the same voiceover in their commercials as for their in-car satnav. At Vodafone, I was responsible for the 'hold music' for callers waiting to be connected with our helplines and customer service advisors. We often ran the music from our latest TV commercial. Luckily, I pressed pause before allowing 'Let It Go' from *Frozen* to be used when I realized that it would play on the bereavement helpline as well as the other lines.

Music plays a part in retail experiences, with an impact ranging from mild (music as a soothing background) to a significant part of the brand experience. Abercrombie & Fitch have moved on from their California-esque surf soundtrack at levels tolerable only to teenage ears to a more inclusive selection and cross-generational decibel level. Canadian fashion retailer Aritzia employ the services of a house DJ to create the right mood in their 80 outlets in North America. Our imaginary Seatown pizzeria aimed at families would probably choose music that appeals to the whole family (including teenagers) and that represents a harmonious vibe with a mediterranean feel rather than a classical Italian repertoire.

The newest thing in auditory branding is the use of voice technology. Alexa and Siri not only directly build the Amazon and Apple brands but also give brands accessed through them a new opportunity to use a characteristic voice in response to web searches. Just one example of this is the California wine grower Gallo, which has recorded hundreds of different responses to create a brand experience for customers accessing its website via voice.

As 5G enables the Internet of Things to become a reality, you might have to start to care about the tone of your kettle's backchat. New technology always creates wonderful new opportunities to build brands.

Delivering all the aspects of a brand's sensorial equities is an undertaking that spans many divisions in a large company, from research scientists to recipe developers to engineers to retail teams. For smaller businesses it might be under the control of one or two people, which makes it much easier. UX (user experience) is the latest jargon for customer experience, and whoever is in charge of the brand needs to remember that the X can and should be delivered by all five senses.

California wine grower Gallo has recorded hundreds of different responses to create a brand experience for customers accessing its website via voice.

CHAPTER 16

Aligning your product and service design with the brand

A brand comprises both product or service and reputation. The product is a such a fundamental part that a whole book could probably barely do justice to the topic of product and service design. As this is a book about brands, I am going to restrict this chapter mostly to the principles of how to ensure that product and service design and innovation add value to the brand and should flow from the brand strategy. It is so common these days to decouple product from brand, and this is simply madness in my opinion. The product is what the customer buys, and will, more than anything else, drive reputation.

Interestingly, a number of scandals affecting the reputation of companies have erupted over the years, ranging from the (non)payment of corporate taxes, to the use of child labour to, in VW's case, emissions testing. In my experience, the aspect of reputation that most impacts customer behaviour and sales is where the matter actually affects the product the customer gets. The scandal of benzene in Perrier water, the horsemeat found in popular brands of lasagne in the UK and the dubbing of jewellery sold by Ratners as 'crap' by the firm's CEO all brought those brands to their knees. Yet when I was at Mondelez (then Kraft) and we acquired Cadbury, we noted no impact on sales whatsoever despite the unpopularity of the takeover and the unjustified vilification of the American company on British TV. Customers do care about the products they buy. And they also care about the ethics and practices of the companies, especially

> The aspect of reputation that most impacts customer behaviour and sales is where the matter actually affects the product.

younger customers. However, their behaviour is much more likely to follow the product or service than anything else. The product or service matters the most.

Mostly, in real life, companies start with a product or service and then figure out their brand. This work might then involve sharpening the existing product to make sure everything is congruent and mutually reinforcing. Or it might be time for new products to be invented, and they should be invented with the brand and customer needs in mind.

Let's start with defining or refining the product or service design – which you should do anyway before embarking on an innovation plan. And for the rest of the chapter, for product and service, I'm just going to say product.

Defining your product design and key equities

As described earlier in the book, the origins of the first product often inform the ethos of the company: the generosity of the glass and a half of milk in Cadbury Dairy Milk, Airbnb's focus on unique homes and local experiences, or Google's simple UX (tech speak for user experience!).

Going product-up rather than brand-down is a good approach where you have a big range of products. You have to find something you can apply across that range so it's sensible to look here first, as a brand-down approach might miss something vital to a particular variant or category.

Do a product review. Get everything out on the table and discuss everything with a cross-functional team – engineers, salespeople, your market research people if you have them. Or if you are a small business, the people that make your product and the people that serve the customers. Your aim is to identify a small number of characteristics of the product or the range that make the brand tick. What do you or your engineers or scientists love about the product and what does the customer love and value? What were the products like when sales were great? Make a list of key features and benefits and then check how important they are and whether each is consonant with the overall brand theme and right to win. If you find huge dissonances between the theme or right to win and things that matter to the customer which drove success, you might have to rethink the brand strategy. Then pick the features and benefits

Make a list of key features and benefits and then check how important they are.

that matter, that are common to the product range, or could be, and that are congruent with the brand. Try to keep to a few… I'd say more than seven and you aren't making strategic choices. And then make any necessary changes to the products over a sensible timescale, and either eliminate or don't invest in features that didn't make the list.

Dove's product philosophy

Take the example of Dove. Our brand theme was Honest Beauty, our differentiation was the use of Real Women in our advertising, and our right to win was Deliver our Promises. At this stage of redefining the brand, we made a great many products: the iconic bar, shower gels, body lotion, deodorant, facecare (mainly in Japan) and haircare. We needed something that united all these categories and that could inspire the teams in new product development (NPD). We wanted to avoid the use of emotive ingredients – those ingredients often cited on packaging as delivering performance but that are not contained in amounts sufficient to deliver a benefit.

But we needed to say what we were, not just what we were not. 'One quarter cleansing cream' had been a major part of the brand since it launched in 1957. In fact, this claim was repeated a total of six times in the 1960s launch TV spot and the words 'cream' or 'creamy' were mentioned a further eight times. David Ogilvy, whose first ever TV commercial this was, had been advised by his pal Bill Bernbach of DDB that the best way to succeed in this nascent advertising medium was repetition. Also included were images of pouring cream… well, why would you not? See, say, repeat! When we reviewed successful ads and moments in the brand's history, this one quarter cleansing (which later evolved into 'moisturizing') claim and the 'pour shot' had aligned with successful products and successful ads. And white, creamy products had succeeded far better than others, such as the pink bar. Customers told us that the whiteness and purity of the product meant a lot to them, and not just because it went with their bathrooms. So whiteness, creaminess and a moisturizing effect were core product equities that the brand team decided must be retained. Additionally, there was a history of professional endorsement by dermatologists recommending Dove for its kindness to sensitive skin. And this aspect had also propelled the brand forward and was an important equity to retain.

However, we were all under no illusion that the beauty and skincare category was highly performance driven. Given that we had decided to be honest and not to use emotive ingredients, we had to be clear that we wanted products that performed. Science will tell you that there are three ways to maintain beautiful skin: keep out of the sun, don't smoke, and moisturize. And that's where Dove would be honest, in that the products would really work and not be based on puffery and fake claims. We engaged with the NPD team and with design agency Seymourpowell to build on past successes but also to define this still further. To inspire the scientists in the NPD team about Honest Beauty, the Dove brand team started by asking them to agree that if they could not wholeheartedly recommend a product they invented to the women they loved, the company would not make it. The event involved the individuals who normally went to work in white coats talking about their mums, sisters, friends, wives and girlfriends. Once we had landed their commitment to this 'product philosophy', we worked with them to underpin it with tangible product features that would apply to each and every product that the brand would make in the future – the product DNA. We created a beautiful hardback book to evoke every aspect, with sections on each; all connected to the brand's overall promise of Honest Beauty.

Starting with the brand to drive the product or service design
If you are new, or have a single product or a relatively small range of products with similar benefits, then starting with the brand is sensible. Assuming you have figured out your brand, it's a simple question of asking what aspects of your current products best fulfil the brand theme and the right to win. Are any unhelpful and should go? When we reviewed the Milka brand, we decided that Alpine milk was a big quality marker and therefore Milka chocolate should always be made with Alpine milk. We should deprioritize any dark chocolate variants, because creamy and soothing was a core product equity.

Lush, the global beauty brand, are avid about sustainability and they train their store staff to find products that are right for each individual customer, as not doing so leads to waste. Other beauty companies will try to sell you as much as you will buy, so Lush's approach really marries with their ethical credentials. They also led the market in creating 'naked products', such as bars of shampoo with no packaging.

Lush – Naked Products support ethical credentials including fighting animal testing, ethical buying, 100% vegetarian ingredients, hand-made products and 'naked' packaging. Clockwise from top left: foundation, lipstick, bath bomb, shower gel, shampoo bar and bath oil.

In the example of our Seatown pizzeria, it has been decided to make wood-fired pizzas. This company we've invented has thought through its brand strategy ahead of opening, and so it can create a product range and service to support its brand theme of the Creates Joyful Togetherness. Customizable pizzas will be the product that can deliver this brilliantly. The service offer that is congruent with this theme is to allow children to 'create your own pizza' on a tablet. If they want to, of course!

Innovation

When you have defined the key qualities of your product or service and ensured these are congruent with the brand, you will reach a stage when you need a plan for innovation. In big companies this is a highly structured process, generally with a series of key 'gates' of approval, as innovation at scale can be costly in labour costs or retooling factories. All innovation programmes tend to follow eight or so stages: problem or opportunity definition; estimate of the 'size of the prize'; ideation; customer evaluation of concepts; concept finalization and selection; product development; product testing. The variations in process and methodology are huge, but most companies' thinking goes through these phases, at scale with a full R&D, or for craft-scale businesses, asking friends and family to try the new thing out.

The best innovations identify an unmet customer need and then find a way to fulfil it.

Defining that problem or opportunity is, of course, fundamental and the best innovations identify an unmet customer need and then find a way to fulfil it. Sometimes the innovations are very practical or even prosaic, arising from something the matter with your existing product.

One such example I was involved with at Mondelez involved Philadelphia cream cheese. We had identified that frequency of use was declining. When we looked into it, we discovered that this was because customers often threw away a proportion of the product uneaten because after one or two uses and a week or more open in the fridge, the cream cheese would develop mould. They were more and more inclined only to buy the product when they were sure it would not go to waste, so they were doing so less and less often. A resealable lid would solve the problem, but the cost of retooling several factories to make this new packaging ran to nearly tens of millions of dollars.

The business case was made because the loss of sales we would expect without doing so could be modelled to demonstrate the return on that investment. Sales of Philadelphia amount to close to $1 billion in annual sales in Europe, so that investment made sense despite costing millions.

Blue-sky innovation

It's much more fun when you are looking not to fix problems but to identify something newly emerging, or more 'blue-sky' opportunities for growth. You should still start with a clear definition of the opportunity or problem, but finding out what you don't know in order to define that opportunity is one of the most genuinely exciting parts of brand building. But how do you identify those things?

Henry Ford, the inventor of mass-produced motor vehicles, famously said, 'if I'd asked people what they wanted they'd have said faster horses', which to some degree undermines the principle of customer-led innovation. It is true that it is unproductive to ask the customer to do your job for you and tell you exactly what they want that doesn't exist. But observing customer trends and customer behaviour does lead to major innovations. And then you need to connect an emerging or nascent desire with the brand.

Henry Ford famously said, 'if I'd asked people what they wanted they'd have said faster horses'.

There are many ways to identify customer trends. The unifying theme is to look for what is starting to happen with people, figure out the trend and how your brand could capitalize on it. Then ask customers what they think of your ideas before going into production. Digital businesses can easily beta test, usually with a product that is 80 per cent right, with thousands of customers who sign up to be part of a testing panel. Many digital businesses have a 'fail forward fast' ethos, by which they prefer to get products out quickly, see if they work, and learn and fix or withdraw and move on if they don't, rather than conservatively testing and perfecting before bringing something to market. This is because the cost of developing new digital products is relatively inexpensive compared with getting a factory to produce enough physical product for a huge number of people to try.

Whatever your approach, there are several places companies typically look for inspiration.

Emerging product trends

Looking at what start-ups are doing is very common. You may spot clusters of innovations that have either the same tech underpinning different offers or are representative of serving the same underlying customer need. How you source this intelligence varies. You can do a clever search on Google based on something you have noticed or picked up, or look at academic papers, for instance. There are agencies you can commission: a major global food company I know asked a specialist insights company to geotag street food markets and listen to social media conversations to spot what new food and drinks were on offer and whether people were enjoying them. Scanning a market for what premium brands are offering if you are a mass-market brand is also popular. Before we cracked down on the use of emotive ingredients, Dove launched a range of products containing pure silk, as this was the latest skincare ingredient promoted by niche beauty brands. This democratization often inspires innovation.

Global market research company Hall & Partners spotted how two companies had used AI to support retail sales in clothes shopping and sanitary protection product delivery. They noted an emerging trend, which they called 'a-commerce' (augmented commerce). Bigger players are now using it, including Walmart with a shopping concierge service they call Jetblack.

Leading-edge markets

Some global markets are more evolved in a particular category. For example, South Korea is very advanced in mobile telephony, and many mobile networks and handset providers look to see what is happening there for inspiration. And some markets leap technologies. Many areas of rural Africa where desktop computers never gained critical mass went straight to mobile. The Vodafone Foundation, which supports projects that use technology to deliver public benefit wherever it trades as a brand, developed a way to create a digital bus ticket for women in these areas to travel to hospital. They were then able to get treatment for a common cause of incontinence, a condition that resulted in them being ostracized by their community.

A major global food company asked a specialist insights company to geotag street food markets.

Emerging legislative trends

While new legislation generally inspires doom in the heart of organizations, necessity really can be the mother of invention here. Governments' appetite for reducing sugar in food, with sugar taxes popping up all around the world, has led to companies designing, or redesigning, their products to contain less of this ingredient. GDPR (General Data Protection Regulation, new laws that give customers more control over how their data is used) has prevented charities sending unsolicited requests for donations. Many charities are having to innovate to rebuild their so-called 'marketable universe' – for example, the British Heart Foundation offered a free 'glow in the dark' children's wall poster of the circulatory system. Recipients were asked if they would like to opt in to receive future marketing and more than half said they would. This 'give–get' model is a new one for charity marketing, and no doubt we will see many inspiring examples from the sector in future.

Sometimes the connection is less direct. When working for an IT company, I looked at the key drivers of the need for software development, and we identified that legislation was a key factor. So we looked at the business categories that were particularly affected by forthcoming legislation and used this to create a focused strategy for the sales force. The construction and finance categories were top of our list at the time.

Emerging consumer trends

Obviously, one can simply find out what customers are doing that is new or emerging. There are companies that make good money identifying what is going on in the world with people and selling this intelligence to larger organizations. Mintel are one of the longest-established specialists in this, but the big consultancy firms such as McKinsey and Deloitte also publish reports. WGSN specializes in consumer goods and design, and there are many other specialist companies, especially in fashion, luxury and digital. You can buy syndicated studies from such companies or request a bespoke analysis. Or you can get on Google yourself and find free reports and webinars or read newspaper reports of how we are all going to hell in a handcart according to the latest research. My best advice is to trust your gut and a few of your own conversations with your customers or prospective customers to assess the validity and likely permanence of any of these trends. If they feel weird and wacky and headline-grabbing to you, they probably are, so I would not be betting my farm on these kinds of things. There is a rule of thumb that any new customer behaviour that lasts for six months and that people like doing will probably stick.

Any new customer behaviour that lasts for six months and that people like doing will probably stick.

Possibly one of the most perfect examples of emerging customer needs aligning with a brand vision is Microsoft Teams. Teams was unveiled at the end of 2016 after beta testing with 50,000 users. By March 2017, 125,000 people were using it; by July 2019, 13 million; and by November 2019, 20 million. Growth that almost every organization on the planet would give their right arm for. In summer 2020, with the COVID-19 pandemic raging round the world, the number had grown to 75 million daily active users. To call this a tailwind is an understatement.

But Teams began life more modestly in response to behaviour that Microsoft observed by monitoring their customers. They saw that people were increasingly trying to work collaboratively online. They began a project to connect together products to facilitate what customers were trying to do for themselves, 'rather like Lego blocks' from what they had already, such as Skype, Office and Cortana. Other companies have also leveraged this customer trend – for example Slack, which launched in 2013.

Teams is the most perfect example of how innovation can both derive from and drive a brand's reputation.

The efforts of the product team working on collaborating tools gained massive traction with the arrival of a new CEO, Satya Nadella, who had joined in 2014. He set out an inspiring refreshed vision for Microsoft, articulating it as follows: 'Empower every person and every organization on the planet to achieve more.' It is a brilliant brand theme. His book *Hit Refresh* tells this brand story as well as recounting the cultural shift he brought about at Microsoft.

Of course, the product bundle that was to become Teams was at the very epicentre of his vision and is the most perfect example of how innovation can both derive from and drive a brand's reputation. And the mission for Teams became even bigger as the product affected the future of work by enabling everything to be in one place for teams in the workplace.

Satya Nadella's vision for teamwork has led to Microsoft's becoming a thought leader in this matter. 'The Art of Teamwork',

MICROSOFT MISSION
Empower every person and every organization on the planet to achieve more

Microsoft's brand strategy flows through into the Teams philosophy and UX.

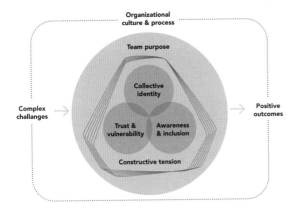

Microsoft's model of outstanding teamwork, promotes team purpose, collective identity, awareness and inclusion, trust and vulnerability, and constructive tension as underpinning high performance. The Teams product is informed by this vision from both a practical and an emotional standpoint. The features added to Teams deliver against this model. They go beyond the practical, such as breakout rooms, whiteboards and document storage, to those features that promote the softer aspects of teamwork. For example, to promote inclusion you can get live transcriptions, which help participants to better follow a meeting when it is not conducted in their native language. Customizable Team Rooms contribute to 'collective identity', and transcripts and recordings enable those who could not attend to catch up afterwards. The developers observed real-life office settings, where you can instinctively tell whether it is the right time to interrupt a colleague by their body language – one feature to help in Teams is a notification when a colleague is working on your project so you can contact them at that time rather than randomly, when it might be an intrusive interruption. They've also added more playful stuff, like the ability to collect money for a colleague's birthday. We await the Secret Santa product!

Underpinning this innovation is a process and structure, whereby the innovation teams at Microsoft cluster customers into 'Groupsonas', a little like the personas or pen portraits depicted in Chapter 4. The 'Groupsonas' are based on types of work: for example the 'Newsroom Groupsona' needs timeliness of information and synchronicity; 'Education and online classrooms' needs software to set, receive, mark and return assignments.

Despite the inevitable generalizations for different customer clusters like this, Nadella's view that every team is different inspires the creation of bespoke solutions as well. For example, Microsoft have just delivered a modified product to Britain's National Health Service, one of the biggest employers in the world. The product is used by 1.3 million staff and Microsoft are learning from those customers to improve the product for them, but also to gain insights for other healthcare providers to improve their capability for everyone. Microsoft created phone-based versions of the Teams app to enable collaboration with front-line health workers, who had only had pagers or walkie-talkies before. They also developed a way to operate with shift work. The learning on this enabled them to offer some of the new functionality to other organizations with similar needs, including the warehouse staff at retailers such as IKEA. I think that the brand theme 'Empower every person and every organization on the planet to achieve more' is wonderfully fulfilled by these innovations, and the democratization of technology beyond the executive layers in an organization makes sense of the 'every person' element of this statement.

As I say, perfect synchronicity between product innovation and brand theme. To which every brand should aspire.

CHAPTER 17

How should you package your brand?

Packaging has defined some brands and made them iconic, including the Tiffany & Co blue box with its white ribbon, the Coca-Cola bottle, the Campbell's soup can, the Heinz ketchup bottle, Toblerone's triangular-shaped box, the squat brown jar of British favourite Marmite and the cubic Chanel No. 5 parfum bottle and stopper. More recently, the boxes of Apple and Amazon are becoming icons of this century. Of Forbes's list of the top 100 digital companies in the world, fewer than half escape the need to consider packaging as a lever for their brands. Those whose product does not have a physical form are mostly B2B consulting or back-end software providers such as Accenture, Fiserve or Salesforce. Of course, there are notable consumer brands that don't have a physical product, including Google, Facebook, Netflix, Airbnb and eBay, but they are exceptions. Companies that are predominantly digital, like PayPal, Microsoft or the many gaming companies, still deliver products in a physical form. So if you're in charge of a brand, chances are you're also going to be in charge of its packaging, and best practice really still belongs to FMCG and luxury brands – with Apple and Amazon as notable exceptions.

For physical brands, packaging can enhance like no other aspect. I confess to first buying Isle of Harris Gin entirely because I adored the bottle. Fortunately, the gin is delicious, and its story of being made with sugar kelp seaweed from the clear waters surrounding the unspoilt Outer Hebridean isle off Scotland helps.

I confess to first buying Isle of Harris Gin entirely because I adored the bottle.

The elements comprising packaging design

Packaging comes in three layers: primary, secondary and tertiary. Primary is the form in which you use the product every time, like a Coke bottle or a tube of toothpaste. Secondary is the container for the first, often needed to house the product neatly on a store shelf or to contain usage instructions, like the box for toothpaste or pills, although it's not always needed. Tertiary packaging refers to the wrapping or container in which it is delivered to its point of distribution. As more and more supermarkets put the tertiary packaging on shelves nowadays, demanding 'shelf-ready packaging' from manufacturers, even this can be an opportunity to build the brand. Each layer is an opportunity, although many brands neglect the third.

Both the physical form and the graphics on the packs can add value to your brand. The form, shape and materials are critical, especially for primary packaging. How does a liquid flow from the hole in a bottle, for example? A slower flow gives more of a premium sense because the product appears to be thicker. Changing the physical form of the packaging once manufactured can be costly, as retooling at factory is required. When we wanted a resealable lid for Philadelphia cheese at Mondelez, as described in Chapter 16, the cost of changing this ran into tens of millions of dollars. There are, of course, many contract packaging firms, and most start-ups will use one rather than buy their own factory! It becomes less of an investment to switch packaging formats if that is how you produce your product. Pack graphics, colour, graphic design and iconography are easier to change, but even then, at scale, it can be costly.

What do you need to consider to build your brand?

This is a book about brands not manufacturing, so I'm going to focus on how to ensure your packaging is on-brand and reputation-enhancing, and, in some cases, how it can alter perceptions of your product.

Like many other aspects of branding, enabling customers to choose is the best place to start when thinking about packaging. Once customers know they want your category of product, you are then in the business of making that choice as easy as possible, and the first thing that helps is enabling them to find your brand effortlessly. Pack recognition is the marketing jargon for

Human brains are hardwired to immediately recognize symbols and visual cues.

this. And here, less is more, despite the way many packs are designed. You need to identify your brand's most immediate and ownable visual signals and design the packaging with as few of these as possible, represented strongly. Human brains are hardwired to immediately recognize symbols and visual cues, road signs being one universal example.

Once your packaging enables your customers to find and choose you, there is the ability of packaging to reinforce both the product experience and the reputation of your brand. Heinz ketchup has built much of its brand reputation on how long it takes its sauce to emerge from the classic bottle. The product could stay the same and the company introduce a bigger neck to the bottle, enabling a freer flow, but they don't. The elegant design and high-quality materials of Apple's packaging helps it to command a premium price and the fact that there are more than 26 million online videos of customers unboxing their products tells you all you need to know about the contribution of packaging to the brand. The products are, of course, beautiful, too.

Five elements determine packaging: shape or form, materials, colour, graphics and brand iconography, and these are in ascending order of ease when it comes to adding uniqueness. If you are an inexpensive brand, using a contract packer, it will be impossible to create uniqueness in the matter of pack shape. Similarly, using packaging contractors will limit the materials you can select, and even if you make it yourself, there will be constraints including technical suitability for transport and storage, and, of course, cost. You will be unconstrained on colour, yes, but unless you trademark it, it can be copied, and even then, other brands can get very, very close. This was a constant source of challenge, including lawsuits, at Cadbury, even though we had trademarked our purple. Most mobile phone boxes are white, in emulation of Apple, although few have the commitment to restraint that preserves Apple's premium feel and uniqueness. Pack graphics can be almost infinitely varied and are therefore ownable. And lastly, there's your brand iconography, including your logo. This is relatively easy to manage, but the temptation is to select too many branding elements or not display them prominently. A common bad habit is to repeat the icon in several places, rather than make that icon impactful. On one of our Milka bar's packs, there were three tiny lilac cows. A customer

Heinz ketchup has built much of its brand reputation on how long it takes its sauce to emerge from the classic bottle.

just won't notice three tiddly cows. With a single big cow, you might have a fighting chance of them realizing the mauve bar of milk chocolate is yours and not the almost identically coloured one made by the supermarket itself. Watch anyone shop for groceries and there is very little scrutinizing of packages: customers mostly grab and go. Packs tend to be covered in verbiage, too. It doesn't help much. At Mondelez, we attached cameras to customers and discovered they read an average of seven words in the whole of their weekly shop. Remember that when designing your pack, and make recognizing your brand visual and as easy as possible.

We attached cameras to customers and discovered they read an average of seven words in the whole of their weekly shop.

Shape or form

At the most elementary level, the pack's shape can preserve the integrity of the goods. Then, the wrong shape or form can add or detract from a brand's reputation. In some research on the Dove packaging, we watched customers grapple with opening the wrapper and box of the bar, becoming frustrated and taking knives and scissors to it. It was an experience that undermined the brand and it prompted us to undertake a complete packaging redesign. Amazon use machine learning to optimize which goods get put in which boxes to ensure the least damage, and their competence is a major brand asset. As well as artificial intelligence, there are also people who earn a living as cardboard engineers, improving packaging from its assembly ergonomics to the way it cradles your precious brand.

At Cadbury, it was the shelf-ready packaging that gave us a big headache. It was known that sales would be better if the bars were not stacked side-on in the boxes but facing the shopper. The barrier to changing to something better was that it would cost millions to retool the factories. More detailed research measured how many people spotted us on shelf – or missed us. We discovered that around two-thirds of shoppers looked at the milk chocolate bars, but only about a quarter spotted Cadbury Dairy Milk. Quantifying this significant potential loss of sales made the case for the investment in front-facing packaging. We didn't need another iconic TV commercial, we needed a new cardboard box, an elastic band and a stick. Sometimes marketing and brand building is no more glamorous than that.

Generally, though, the shape of packaging goes beyond the practical and is an uplifting brand asset. The Coca-Cola bottle with its fluted contours is without doubt a cultural icon. It's been immortalized by Andy Warhol and Salvador Dalí and many other painters and sculptors. It was described by the noted industrial designer Raymond Loewy as 'the perfect liquid wrapper'. It was patented in 1915, has evolved over the past century and inspires the graphic lines on the more ubiquitous can.

When a brand goes back 100 years or more, deconstructing why that shape is 'on-brand' is harder. I would suggest that the 'flow of liquid' described for Coca-Cola evokes refreshment. It's easier to identify a connection between packaging and a brand's strategy in those brought to market more recently. The Isle of Harris Gin bottle's shape is the most evocative element of their packaging (shown opposite), evoking the maritime elements of the Hebridean island where it is made. The blue glass references the colour of the sea in summer and the smooth-edged curves and dimples are reminiscent of the wind-blown sea and sand, or of sea glass worn by the tides. On a more practical note, the bottle mouth has been computer modelled not to spill or drip. I only wish one could say the same of the thousands of teapot and jug manufacturers in the world. But for Isle of Harris Gin, this packaging creates a premium experience and one that 'captures the spirit of the island'.

Iconic pack shapes.

The Coca-Cola bottle was described by the noted industrial designer Raymond Loewy as 'the perfect liquid wrapper'.

Packaging evokes the brand's story.

Toblerone's triangular shape goes back to 1908, and most people believe it evokes the shape of the Alps near Bern in Switzerland, where it is made. However, Theodor Tobler, its inventor's son, claims it was inspired by the triangular shape made by dancers his father saw at the Folies Bergère in Paris! Whatever its provenance, the shape is its most distinctive feature, and is patented. Thankfully, most people will not think of whatever triangles the Parisian dancers presented but of the high quality of Swiss Alpine chocolate when they eat it. Toblerone was one of the brands I struggled with at Mondelez… It is a unique and delicious chocolate (especially in its 4.5 kg bar form!), but the pointy nature of its triangular segments makes it quite a demanding eat, less pleasurable than more rounded forms of chocolate. And we never resolved that tension between its uniqueness and its relevance. It remains, to this day, a great gift, particularly popular for men, but not something you'd select for an everyday treat, the hallmark of bigger-selling brands.

The fragrance market probably makes the best use of pack shapes to express brands, ranging from that restrained classic, Chanel No. 5, to contemporary, apothecary-inspired brands such as Le Labo to more literal expressions such as Jean Paul Gaultier's explicitly erotic Le Beau, Diesel's fist for Only the Brave and the ingot representing Paco Rabanne's 1 Million brand.

Materials

To satisfy the practical requirements such as stability and portability, you will probably have settled on one of the most common materials – paper or board, glass, metal or plastic. Even then, the material can reflect the brand's strategy. One great example of this is Clipper Tea, or Cupper as it is known in Germany. A brand with 'natural' as one of its core equities, it does two things with its packaging. First, it does not bleach its tea bags, so they remain a beige colour, a feature you notice every time you make a cuppa – as the ad below says: 'Say hello to the world's first plastic-free, non-GM, unbleached tea bag'. Second, they use fairly standard card to make their boxes, but print on the 'wrong', more matt side of it, so the colour palette is slightly muted, and the packaging is less glossy and feels more organic. Kit Kat used to wrap the bar first in foil, then in paper. You could isolate

The right packaging material can distinguish a brand.

each finger in the bar by running a fingernail down the foil and breaking a segment of wafer biscuit off without touching the chocolate. This made it a brilliant treat to share and a satisfying experience. Those days are gone, sadly, as in 2001 Nestlé replaced this format with flow-wrap plastic just like every other bar of chocolate. Plastic's advantage is that it is easy to mould, and Evian makes use of this, with the mountain shape of its bottles reflecting the Alpine provenance of the water they contain. Of course, every brand is working hard to reduce its environmental footprint, especially regarding the use of plastics, and no doubt we will see great creativity to come as more and more brands seek new materials to create circular economics. The use of metal tends to be standard with cans and caddies; Jean Paul Gaultier is one of the few brands to use it imaginatively, with a can as secondary packaging as opposed to card, omnipresent in the fragrance category.

Colour

Chapter 13 expands on the importance of colour to a brand. And it's the colour of their packaging that defines many iconic brands; Tiffany, Hermès, Coca-Cola, Veuve Clicquot, Cadbury and Milka to name a few. If you have a brand colour that is ownable, I'd ensure it was dominant on your packaging, especially if you are stocked alongside other brands. It's the aspect that customers notice first when shopping for you. Dove stands out on shelf because of its dominant white colour. Colour also can act as a marker for a whole category. Because so many brands have copied Cadbury's purple, customers looking for milk chocolate will probably look for the section dominated by that colour. Then it's down to the pack graphics and brand icons to help customers find and grab you.

The other matter where pack colours can help customers get the right product is if you have a range of products. A secondary colour can facilitate the selection of different variants. My favourite brand of conditioner does not do this well, and I am always getting home to find I've bought the shampoo by mistake. I then choose to use up the shampoo (which I don't like) rather than go to the trouble of returning it, which then detracts from my nice warm feeling about the brand. This might be irrational, but customers' behaviour often is!

Pack graphics

This is a playpen for designers and can add so much character and desirability to a brand. You are more likely to change your pack graphics than any other aspect of the brand, and the potential outcomes are almost infinite. You will have legal compliance aspects to consider, such as ingredients or health traffic-light issues in some countries, but the rest is all joy. Unless you are a tobacco brand, in which case you have to notify customers about how they might die or harm their unborn babies.

You are more likely to change your pack graphics than any other aspect of the brand.

Even with the unpromising starting point of a cardboard box, Target added a cute dog icon to their most popular sizes, looking as though the dog was driving a van. Amazon have their smiley icon, which reflects the happy feeling you get when a delivery arrives. And I was charmed by the delivery of some Havaiana flip-flops recently, where the inside of the cardboard box they arrived in was brightly coloured with lovely images evoking the spirit of Brazil and the brand. More brands should consider the insides of their delivery boxes.

The pack graphics should of course evoke the brand strategy, both determining and using key visual equities. The variety is

Pack graphics create distinctive brands in one category even with similar pack formats.

infinite, as are brands, but the examples opposite indicate the range that is possible, even in an everyday category such as tea.

Brand icons

The best way to select these icons is to know what symbols the customer associates most strongly with your brand. JKR, the global design agency, figure this out by asking customers to draw the brand. One of their famous case studies was for the Guinness can, with the golden harp featuring strongly in these sketches. JKR then removed almost all other iconography apart from the logo from that can, creating a design that not only was beautiful but also drove a double-digit increase in sales. Why? Mostly, because the customer could find it more easily. Not rocket science – but simplifying often seems to be one of the hardest things to accomplish. Apple are, of course, past masters at it. Microsoft, whose design credentials compared to Apple's have often been lampooned in online videos, have recently upped their

Before

After

The Guinness can: simplify and deploy your icons.

game with their Windows software packaging. It's elegant and unmistakable, and enables distinction between variants.

Briefing for new packaging and ensuring it is on-brand

The place to start when you are seeking new packaging for your brand or bringing a new product to market is, of course, the brand strategy, and the most useful parts are the right to win and the overall brand theme. Knowing who is going to buy or use the product (not always the same thing) is also helpful, as well as any technical detail regarding the physical properties needed to house the product or manufacturing capability. And a review of the packaging of your main competitors should also form part of it. Key visual equities will need to be mandated, and if it is a brand extension, be clear which aspects or icons must be consistent across the range.

The example opposite indicates what should be included in a typical brief to a designer.

Indicative design brief

Packaging is more important when it comes to giving a gift than if you are buying something for yourself. Presentation is everything, and the unwrapping is designed to be a major part of that experience. Ribbons, layers, wrappers. If you are lucky enough to be given a gift from Tiffany, there will potentially be six layers of packaging: the blue carrier bag, the white ribbon, the blue box, a layer of white tissue paper or foam and finally the blue fabric pouch enclosing your item of jewellery. And there are little Ts stamped all over the box and bags, one way of determining if you've been given a fake – best to check, especially if the gift accompanies a proposal of marriage! Consider also the frequently given heart-shaped boxes of chocolates for Valentine's day, from everyday brands like Hershey or Cadbury to the premium brands such as Charbonnel et Walker from the UK or Chicago-based Vosges. In these cases, I suspect that the packaging can cost more than the product. But, to paraphrase another brand's catchphrase, the experience is priceless.

Brand Design Brief

1. Is the scope and purpose of the project to create a new brand, or radically overhaul or refresh an existing one? What has driven this requirement?

2. Who is our customer, what do they think of us and where do they interact with us?

3. What is our brand positioning and strategy?

4. Current visual identity. What is valued and what is not working?

5. List of key competitors, especially those you fear the most.

6. Define the change. What do we want to move 'from' 'to'? What do we need to keep?

7. Brands whose look you aspire to emulate and why, showing key images.

8. Mood board of desired direction.

9. What assets are you looking to refresh?

10. Any sacred cows, trademarked assets, legal compliance?

11. Project timescale, key stakeholder presentations and 'go live' date.

12. Budget, including design fees and production of master assets.

CHAPTER 18

How to keep all this together once you've figured it out

I wouldn't blame you if you needed a lie-down now you've read all this. Creating and curating a brand is actually quite a lot of work, and it's futile to pretend otherwise. But it's rare that you have to do it all in one go. It tends to be more organic than that and it is a creative endeavour that is inspiring and fun. The outcome of all the thinking and creating needs to be captured somewhere so that it can be understood and applied by those who need to bring the brand to life. Companies often describe this document, whether physical or digital, as their 'brand book'. Hence the title of this one, a gag that marketers get immediately – other individuals not so much!

Guidelines need to be written down.

If you are starting work as the new marketing director or brand director of a large company, there will probably be something in place already that may need to be evolved. Or it might be fine and just needs to be better communicated and managed. Vodafone UK had design guidelines and a tone-of-voice guide of random provenance, but little else that gave the brand meaning or explained the thinking. Fortunately, the global team had delivered outstanding design work, but I still needed to add the bits that were missing for the UK, which was mostly about customer understanding, differentiation, brand purpose and the tone of voice. If you are a start-up, you should start with your strategy and then add what you need as the business develops. Whatever the stage of the business or the state of the brand, you do need to capture what is decided as a guide. Even if you are a one-man-band, you will probably forget the name of the perfect subhead font for the navigation tabs on your website! And the minute there are even two of you bringing the brand to life in public, you'll need a set of principles you agree on and can follow. Guidelines need to be written down and this is what they should include:

Brand book contents

Welcome to the world of
Brand X

Everything you need to know to bring our beloved brand to life.

Contents

Furthermore, the guidelines need to be easily at hand for people, whoever and wherever they are, otherwise people will make it up or remember it badly and the brand presentation will get flaky. Most companies these days host all this information on a microsite, which companies like because it is accessible and can be modified cheaply and easily. I think the latter is actually a disadvantage because guidelines shouldn't be changed lightly and wantonly. Making them harder to fiddle with is a good thing. But I'm rather a lone voice on this one. There is something pretty emphatic and permanent about going to print with something! It feels special, significant and real. Which is how an organization should want its brand guidelines to feel. For that reason, I still have heart for a physical brand book. Done well, they are not only useful but respected and cherished. I had a brand book for Oreo on my desk at Mondelez which looked just like the eponymous cookie and everyone who came into my office picked it up and remarked on it. Almost everyone asked if they could have it and some were allowed to receive one.

> **Socking the brand to the organization and keeping it socked takes continuous effort.**

In our new, work-from-anywhere digital culture, physical brand books are rarer and rarer, but most great companies have a digital or online version as an essential part of the marketing toolkit. If the organization can afford it, I'd recommend also presenting new marketers with a physical manifestation of the brand (equivalent to the Oreo cookie) containing the guidelines on a USB stick, or a wall chart summarizing them. Or both. I like something that impresses upon marketers the significance of the brand, and something tangible will do this more than a microsite ever will.

As described in Chapter 10, socking the brand to the organization and keeping it socked takes continuous effort. And the guidelines also need to be communicated and explained to everyone who needs to know them: this is an ongoing programme of work, because people and a company's creative agencies change. Bigger organizations will go even further than this and will have a team of people who can check either pre-emptively or retrospectively every communication to ensure it complies with the guidelines. I had such a team at Vodafone. Sometimes these poor folks are unkindly dubbed the 'Brand Police' and some marketers who like to consider themselves trendy describe such roles and guidelines as outmoded, citing aphorisms such as 'fail forward fast' and 'move fast and break things' as their justification for rule-breaking. The irony is that even the authors of such mantras manage their brands very tightly. Companies from Coca-Cola to LinkedIn to Beats by Dre all have brand guidelines and they are taken very seriously. Whatever you call your guidelines and whatever form they're in, keeping your brand cohesive and, hopefully, magnificent is never going to be old.

Keeping your brand cohesive and, hopefully, magnificent is never going to be old.

Real or virtual, the best brands have brand books.

Part 3: Great brands and why I love them

To be honest, I could fill a whole book with examples of brands that bring themselves to life brilliantly. This is a very personal selection of brands that I admire for specific aspects of brand building. I am sure many readers will think of examples that they prefer. But I hope my choice demonstrates what great looks like, at a minimum. And I hope thinking of your own dissenting examples only serves to deepen your understanding or reignite your passion for brands.

Method

Loved for: Disruptive and gorgeous packaging design in an ugly category

Dove

Loved for: Purpose-led strategy sustained for nearly two decades

Top: Campaign for Real Beauty launched in 2004 and ran in over 70 countries

Bottom: Launch advertising in Europe generated extraordinary amounts of PR

Wrinkled?
Wonderful?

Cuvy thighs, bigger bums, rounder stomachs. What better way to test our firming range?

Top: Real Beauty Sketches: viral campaign released in 2013, with over 180 million views

Bottom: Charitable support since 2004

Dove Real Beauty Sketches
Do you see the beauty in yourself? If someone asked you to describe yourself, what would you say? Our body image takes such a battering that feeling beautiful can be hard – in fact, sometimes we just can't see beauty in ourselves at all. We think our self-esteem is in serious need of a boost.

Welcome to the Dove Self-Esteem Project
At Dove, we believe that no young person should be held back from reaching their full potential – but in the UK and Ireland, 9 out of every 10 girls with low body esteem put their health at risk by not seeing a doctor or skipping meals. Since 2004, Dove has been building self-esteem in young people – and by 2030, we'll have helped ¼ billion through our educational programmes.

Loaf

Loved for: Fresh, informal and British tone and manner

Welcome to our loaf shack!

Wodge Modular Sofa

If this sofa were a cake, it would be one where only whopping great slices would be allowed. None of that "Just a tiny bit" malarkey.

Sugar Bum Sofa

Google

Loved for: Unmistakable visual identity and outstanding management of it over time

Over twenty years of consistency: Early days in 1998

A refined example that lasted from 1999 from 2015

A more dramatic change in 2015

Google Doodles, from top: 100th birthday of American artist Mary Blair, 76th birthday of Mr. Men's creator and appropriate tribute to the anniversary of the world-wide-web

App icons

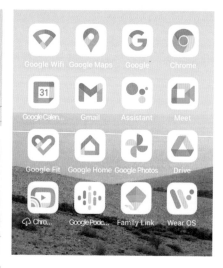

Dolce&Gabbana

Loved for: Vibrant signature look that celebrates characterful women and the female form

Apple

Loved for: 'Come and get me' allure engendered by beauty and scarcity

Nike

Loved for: 30 years of fearless advertising

'Believe in something, even if it means sacrificing everything.'
Colin Kaepernick (2018)

Land Rover

Loved for: Over 70 years of doing one thing brilliantly

1 Series 1 1948
2 Series 2 1958
3 Range Rover
  1st generation 1970

4 Discovery 1989
5 Defender 1990
6 Freelander 1997
7 Range Rover L322 2001

8 Evoque 2011
9 Velar 2017
10 Discovery Sport 2019

6

7

8

9

10

Microsoft

Loved for: The utility and innovation that has driven mass adoption

Top: Integrated suite of products

Centre left: PowerPoint: the ubiquitous, user-friendly presentation platform

Centre right: PowerPoint in action: the backdrop to my professional life. Here with retail guru Mary Portas

Bottom: More inclusive UX on Microsoft Teams

Part 4: Branding toolkit

This section gives you one toolkit to help you figure out your brand's strategy and key elements of how to execute it. And, as they say on the BBC to avoid promoting any one entity over another, 'other toolkits are available'. These are the tools which I find to be excellent – either because I have used them myself or simply because I have much faith in them.

Any tool is only as good as the person using it… so although these guidelines do not guarantee success, I hope they help you to think about the right things, making your brand a little bolder and better.

To illustrate how to wield these guidelines in practice, we've chosen Seatown's fictional pizzeria. With many thanks to Alyssa and Charlie, who delivered the artistic elements needed to bring it to life.

1. Customer definition and insight Template

Who are we targeting?

Who are we not targeting?

WHAT DO CONSUMERS	LIFE	CATEGORY	BRAND
DO			
THINK/ BELIEVE/ FEEL			
WANT			
KEY INSIGHT:			

Guidance notes

It is just as important to define who you are not targeting – don't leave this section blank. If you seek to appeal to everyone, you'll appeal to noone. You can discriminate between customer types by attitude, behaviour or demographics. But discriminate you must!

The table should, first of all, make it clear which aspect of life is relevant and which category you are in. Then you should be able to be read across and down and link each box with 'because' or 'and so' – and the narrative must make sense. The best insight will be found somewhere in the middle of the table. If you choose too big an insight, i.e. too connected to life and too far to the left, your claims may end up overblown. Too far to the right and they will be a little limited. Going up and down between 'do', 'think' and 'want' is more optional, but you might end up with a rather functional outcome if you stay at the top of the table. The exercise ensures you get the balance right.

When this is completed, you should be able to recognize the humans you describe and the language should be plain and simple. If it feels contrived or strange, you probably have more work to do.

Worked example for Pizza United

Who are we targeting?
Families with children (tiny to teenagers) on holiday in the town, having one of the more treaty meals out during their stay: a birthday or celebrating the end of their vacation.
Who are we not targeting?
Local residents. Of course they are welcome, but they are not our main source of business.

WHAT DO CONSUMERS	FAMILY LIFE	HOLIDAY DINING	BRAND
DO	Choose carefully when it comes to things for their family.	When eating out, they research options to ensure that everyone's dietary needs and preferences are catered for.	Don't know the restaurant, so look online at several options .... Pizza being a promising start, they then dig deeper, checking out the menu and customer reviews.
THINK/ BELIEVE/ FEEL	Time spent with my family is the most precious of all.	When the kids are happy, everyone is happy (and when the kids are miserable, everyone else is twice as miserable).	Pizza United massively increases the chances of a wonderful evening. Everyone loves pizza and everyone can have their favourite.
WANT	Those precious times to be wonderful.	A joyful occasion that will make a happy holiday memory.	Everyone to be delighted with their food.

KEY INSIGHT: When the kids are happy, everyone is happy.

Notes to the example

In addition to finding the key insight regarding the motivation of our lovely customer here, some other insights emerge from this exercise. The lack of awareness and experience of restaurants in the context of a family's first visit to a holiday town becomes very obvious when filling out this grid. Lack of awareness and understanding would also be the case for any new business or new product launch. This customer understanding will lead to a number of executional decisions to help the business. For example, having the word 'pizza' in its name should increase customer consideration, because strangers to the town immediately know what is offered (and that this is a suitable restaurant for families, because everyone likes a pizza), whereas another more enigmatic option, such as 'Popolare', would not.

2. Competition and differentiation Template

ASPECT	COMPETITOR 1	COMPETITOR 2	COMPETITOR 3	COMPETITOR 4	COMPETITOR 5
LOGO					
SLOGAN					
POSITIONING OR MAIN CLAIM					
PRODUCT					
COLOURS					
TYPE, LOOK AND FEEL					
TONE AND MANNER					
BEHAVIOUR					

Differentiation: What does the competition do? Then a clear statement of how you are different.

Guidance notes

The list of aspects can cover many things that are relevant to the category in which you are competing. Don't make your list too long, though… 6–12 things is enough.

It doesn't need to be an exhaustive list of every single competitor in the area, but should comprise those organizations which your customer regularly chooses instead of you, or might choose if it's a new product. To make that selection, just imagine who you expect to take business away from. Don't be afraid to include a market leader or two, even if you are small… you'll learn a lot from what they have done and it won't serve you if you accidentally copy them. Local businesses where big chains don't compete may not need to do this, but will need to check them out to ensure you're not close

Worked example for Pizza United

ASPECT	7 BONE BURGER	THE FISH PLAICE	THE INN ON THE BEACH	PIER HEAD	LA TRATTORIA
LOGO	7bone			PIER HEAD Food & Drink	la Trattoria
SLOGAN	Servin' up burgers, beers and lols	Fish and potatoes at their finest	None	None. No website.	Benvenuto da la Trattoria
POSITIONING OR MAIN CLAIM	American comfort food, in a laid-back speakeasy joint.	Good quality – family run.	Beachside location makes it a great place to unwind.	Nothing overt. Local seafood.	The leading local Italian restaurant. Authentic Italian.
PRODUCT	Burgers, smoked hot dogs, cocktails, beer, cider.	Fish and chips.	Seafood, fish, pub classics.	Locally sourced seafood. With sophisticated recipes.	Traditional Italian cuisine.
COLOURS	Yellow, fuchsia, black and white.	Blue and white.	Navy, white, teal, blue.	Blue and white.	Red, white and green of the Italian flag.
TYPE, LOOK AND FEEL	Old school typewriter plus handwriting. Messy.	Playful, friendly, fish iconography.	Modern, sans serif. Mixture across assets.	Modern, clean. Seafood iconography.	Handwritten script. Nondescript font.
TONE AND MANNER	Down home frat house meets hipster.	Personal. Friendly. People behind the brand.	Not much personality evident.	Not much personality evident. Friendly, some humour.	Friendly, personable.
BEHAVIOUR	None declared or evident.	Responsible sourcing.	Nothing evident.	Local sourcing.	Food prepared and cooked on the premises.

Differentiation: Naffness and seaside clichés abound. We are a class act in a class of our own.

Notes to the example

enough to get sued! I've done up to 20 competitors several times delivering this framework. In my view of all the templates, it is the most valuable to do, even if it is quite a lot of work and feels a bit daunting.

Having viewed what is out there, choose how you are going to be different overall. This is a big overarching theme, one which inspires action; a memorable headline, not a detail.

The commentary is the opinion of the author, in order to illustrate how such an exercise might look in real life. As is often the case for smaller businesses, competitors' positioning and brand expression is not fully formed. In this example, 7 Bone Burger is a good example of a small restaurant chain, where the branding is clear and brought to life well.

3. Right to win Template

Founding ethos
Why was the business started in the first place and what was it about
the founders that made it succeed?

Highs in its business history
Look at the full history of the company – at triumphs (when the brand was growing or
gaining market share) and disasters (when it was shrinking or when it made big mistakes).
A theme may emerge.

Values
What is the company like when it is at its best? What are the people like when at their best?
This is an especially rich area for brands delivered in a large part by people.

Best ads
Some of the ads that drove the best results. What were they saying, why did they work?

The myths and legends
What stories do people tell about the company to illustrate how great it was
or how it succeeded against the odds?

Lessons from brand disasters
What happened when the company lost its way and even was at risk? What was missing?

Right to win: A short summary statement of what you offer the customer

Guidance notes

This is a suggested list of aspects to review to find
a truth about your brand that will enable you to
succeed with your customer. A unifying theme will
emerge. It then needs to be articulated in a very
short and single-minded way. No lists!! It doesn't
matter if this is unique to your brand, but it should
be something your brand does particularly well.
New brands will draw on their founding ethos.

Worked example for Pizza United

Founding ethos

In our early 50s, with our kids at university, we felt we could realize a long-held ambition to open our own restaurant. We had an appetite to make something a little bit premium. But what? We lived by the seaside and knew that tourists were the main driver of our home town's economy. Visitors were mainly families or retirees. The older couples we saw seemed to have lots of choice, but we felt there wasn't anything much for the families at the nicer end of the market. So we decided to aim our new restaurant at this group. Most had kids, typically aged 5 to 15.

As parents, we often found ourselves eating somewhere we didn't really like, just to keep the kids happy. For day-to-day meals out, this wasn't such a big deal….but for those special meals, finding somewhere we all liked seemed to be an impossible dream. When we took holidays, we always had a special meal the night before we went home or if the holiday coincided with a birthday or the anniversary of a special occasion. We often struggled to find something… plenty of cheap eats, but not much that had an ambience and food that the kids also liked. We often used to say to our friends 'when you eat out with kids, your fate is to go downmarket'. So we decided that we would resolve that conundrum for parents.

We remembered a family meal we had had in Florence, in an old-style family restaurant, when the kids were 8 and 10 years old. The 'nonna' let our kids choose their toppings and help make the pizza… and the patron plied us with red wine. When we sat down together, we were like the families eating out that you see in magazines.

And when some of our kids became teenagers, a whole new war erupted when the older ones refused to eat anywhere 'kiddish'. So our restaurant had to have an adult style. And we had no desire to create a theme park to appeal only to our youngest visitors.

Our desk research told us that pizza is the food no one dislikes and is the second most popular in the western world. Also, stone-baked pizza was a big food trend. And to our delight, there was no restaurant in our town devoted to pizza, and very few places that were upmarket but that kids might also enjoy. Bingo… we had our idea and our killer offer! Stone-baked artisanal pizza, but fully customizable …. plus the kids can supervise the chef adding the toppings. More research uncovered evidence that if kids create food, they are more likely to eat it and enjoy it. This would be a place where the kids would be happy and so would everyone else.

Right to win: fully customizable pizza

Notes to the example

For new entities, the founding ethos is pretty much the only place to look for the right to win. Values can also work in this instance, but it will most likely be the founders' values or those they wish to create.

4. Cultural context Template

CANDIDATE TREND	IMPACT ON CUSTOMER	CONNECTION TO BRAND	EVIDENCE THAT IT IS SUSTAINABLE
TREND 1			
TREND 2			
TREND 3			
TREND 4			
Cultural context: Articulate the trend in the most powerful way.			

Guidance notes

You should consider more trends than those you've shortlisted. Some will not be useful because they will not be relevant to the customer or the brand, or because they are a fad. You should build your brand to last, so this trend should be one that you expect to be around for years to come. If a trend is new, you should evidence that it is here to stay.

Those that fulfil these criteria can then be considered and you should choose the one that has the biggest impact on the customer and strongest connection with the brand. Further aspects to aid selection are a) the scope for PR and social media conversations where the brand can have a legitimate, valid point of view and

Worked example for Pizza United

CANDIDATE TREND	IMPACT ON CUSTOMER	CONNECTION TO BRAND	EVIDENCE THAT IT IS SUSTAINABLE
INFORMAL EATING	Easier to take kids out to eat in informal settings.	Pizza is not 'fine dining'.	Many famous fine-dining chefs are creating more casual restaurant chains.
ARTISANAL FOOD	More confident in unprocessed food with fewer nasty ingredients.	Made on site and in front of you.	Data supports the growth of the category over the last 20 years.
DIETARY NEEDS	Every gathering is fraught with dietary requirements – there's always someone with something that needs managing.	Everyone's dietary need can be accommodated when each creates their own.	Food allergy stats show allergies on the rise. Vegetarianism and veganism on the rise.
LOCAL SOURCING	Feel good that their food choices tread lightly on the planet.	Local ingredients where possible.	Data shows the number of restaurants offering it are on the rise.

Cultural context: There is an explosion of food needs and demands.

b) if competitors are making mileage or not from any of the aspects, in which case you might choose an alternative.

Notes to the example

The dietary needs trend was felt to have the biggest impact on our customer and had the strongest connection with the brand. Artisanal and informal trends have the weakest impact on the customer and less connection to the brand. Local sourcing could be a good option but is a feature of competitor offers.

5. Brand theme and manifesto Template

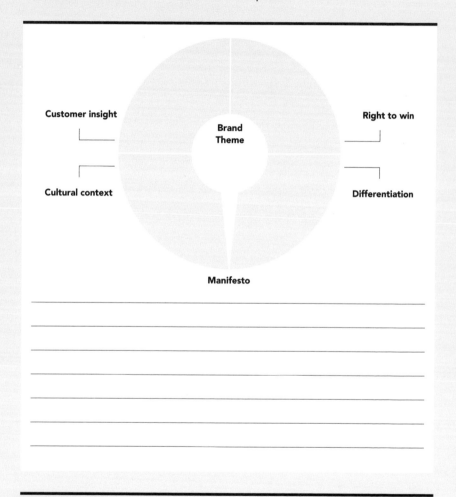

Customer insight

Brand Theme

Right to win

Cultural context

Differentiation

Manifesto

Guidance notes

By completing the previous worksheets you will have generated the four levers. Then you need to connect them with an overarching theme that is an offer to the customer or reflects the brands soul. The theme should connect logically with each of the levers. As this work progresses, there may be some modifications to everything but the customer insight (which is not really in the brand's gift to modify). The aim is to make the logic work seamlessly, especially between the theme and the right to win. You should be able to link these two elements using the word 'because'. This can take quite a lot of work and honing to get it short and sharp!

The manifesto is a longer, more poetic version of the brand theme, which you would share with your organization.

Worked example for Pizza United

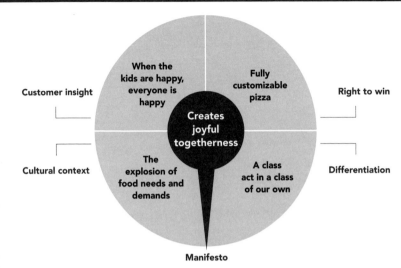

Customer insight

When the kids are happy, everyone is happy

Right to win

Fully customizable pizza

Creates joyful togetherness

Cultural context

The explosion of food needs and demands

Differentiation

A class act in a class of our own

Manifesto

We've seen the pictures of families eating in the holiday magazines and we yearn for that in real life, because it's hard to cater for everyone these days. What it takes for happiness to erupt is for everyone to get their favourite meal and to have fun at the same time. Everyone loves pizza… and everyone has their favourite. At Pizza United, we let everyone choose exactly what they want … and what they need. From a gluten-intolerant vegan teenager, to a toddler who cries at the sight of a tomato, to a dad who can never get enough chili and pepperoni, we cater for everyone with our customizable offering. Whatever you want, you can have it, as long as it's a pizza! And if you like, you can help the chef make it even more to your taste by specifying how much and where you want every ingredient. We believe that creating food can be fun for all ages, but we don't like gimmicks, and our restaurant has just enough sophistication for adults to be happy.

We want our restaurant to look just like the pictures in magazines. So everyone in our restaurant will go the extra mile to create occasions when families enjoy harmony, joy and togetherness, making memories to cherish.

Notes to the example – how we came by the name

We came up with Pizza United during the process of figuring out this strategy and imagining our customers picking a restaurant in a town they don't know that well. Visitors know immediately from the name that it is a pizza restaurant. And it reflects the strategic theme of togetherness. No one will be embarrassed by not being able to pronounce it, and it is cool enough to impress the average teenager, and it differentiates by avoiding Italian and seaside clichés.

6. Brand behaviour Template

BRAND ASPECT	WHAT WE DO	WHAT WE DON'T DO
ASPECT 1		
ASPECT 2		
ASPECT 3		
ASPECT 4		
ASPECT 5		
ASPECT 6		

Guidance notes

This should cover those operational aspects of the brand that directly build on, or could detract from, the overall positioning or theme. Think of them as proof points for your brand theme. Any aspects can be included, but to consider candidates for the list, think about how your product is made, how your service is delivered, where you are based or distributed, how you treat your customers and employees, and how your marketing communications and promotions are done. Your operational manuals will contain many procedures and processes, but 'Brand Behaviour' should list a few carefully chosen actions that build the brand. You don't need too many – 3 to 10 should do it, and

Worked example for Pizza United

BRAND ASPECT	WHAT WE DO	WHAT WE DON'T DO
CUSTOMIZ-ABILITY	Let customers choose exactly the pizza they want, either on iPads or with fuzzy felt ingredients. The kid can take their creation to the chef and see it made if they want too.	If it won't fit in the oven or features an obscene design, that's when we say no.
PRODUCT QUALITY	Use wholesome ingredients	No artificial additives unless mandated for health and safety reasons.
DIETARY NEEDS	All staff are trained and have to pass a test every six months. We have an allergy preparation section. We have vegan and 'free from' options. We operate a nut free environment.	We don't have any nuts in the house. It's the only favourite ingredient we don't supply because we put safety first.
STAFF RECRUITMENT	One of the interviewers for our staff will be a child. We prefer to employ people who have had kids.	Allow people to continue to work for us if they get grumpy with our customers' children.
TRADING HOURS	We start serving dinner at 5pm.	
GREETING THE CUSTOMER	Offer the parents a big glass of wine as soon as they sit down.	

they are the sort of thing that all the employees must know, remember and live. The main message about your brand will be based on the brand theme and the right to win. Brand behaviours are more behind-the-scenes aspects, or things the customer can discover if they choose to find out more about you.

Notes to the example

These six things would make a good start to build the Pizza United brand. Such aspects evolve over time, but should be kept a simple as possible.

7. **Visual equities** Worked example for Pizza United

Logo and variants
Brand icons
Primary colour palette
Secondary colour palette

Design ethos
Photographic style
Typography

Notes to the example
Left is the list of assets you will need.
In the full brand guidelines much more narrative and detail would be provided.

The main logo: our 'U' references a pizza crust, which we also use to represent a glass of wine. And it looks smiley. Which we are. Logo variants: reversed out of a darker background.

Brand icons: the pizza (with the crust that gives us our U), wine glasses and building your own.

Primary and secondary colour palettes.

e99809

80324c

Colour Palette Inspo

fee69e

f2b6b6

c2272d

Boradacre

Aa Bb Cc Dd Ee Ff Gg Hh Ii Jj Kk Ll
Mm Nn Oo Pp Qq Rr Ss Tt Uu Vv
Ww Xx Yy Zz

Cobert

Aa Bb Cc Dd Ee Ff Gg Hh Ii Jj Kk Ll Mm
Nn Oo Pp Qq Rr Ss Tt Uu Vv Ww Xx
Yy Zz

Typography: headline and body copy fonts.

Photographic style: muted tones, evening sunshine, evocative of Mediterranean warmth...

Sample visual equities in use for Pizza United

8. Sensory equities Template

SENSE	RATIONALE	EXECUTION
SOUND		
SMELL		
TASTE		
FEEL		

Guidance notes

Not all will apply to your brand... omit as necessary.

The rationale should explain the connection between the equities and the brand positioning, as well as the execution and what will deliver them. These are the headlines for the more detailed instructions on execution, such as HR for staff training, the property manager for the fragrance at retail, or IT for sound effects in the app, etc. This is where the brand thinking leads and connects to the operational delivery.

Worked example for Pizza United

SENSE	RATIONALE	EXECUTION
SOUND	Happy, harmonious, holiday. Class act.	Happy, up-beat, chilled out… Buddha Bar/Ibiza.
SMELL	Possibly the most popular smell in the world.	Freshly baked (ciabatta) bread (site bread oven near the door vents to street).
TASTE	Wholesome but indulgent.	Fresh-tasting yumminess from fresh ingredients.
FEEL	Joyful and welcoming.	Sunny, warm colours, warm temperature and a warm welcome.

Notes to the example

Each of these aspects would be detailed fully in the design and build specification for the restaurant fit-out and the staff training manual. For any food brand, the taste section will be much expanded in conjunction with the chef, guided by this theme and detailed in the product DNA part of the brand thinking.

9. Tone and manner Template

Customer insight   BRAND THEME   Differentiation

Would speak like this...	....and not like this
Inspiring summation:	

Guidance notes

Most tone-of-voice guides do not connect to the strategic theme, customer insight or differentiation, so it's difficult to see how they help the brand to stand for anything. Consider how a person who exemplifies these aspects of your brand might talk in order to select adjectives that define the tone and manner. In many cases, the adjectives used are very anodyne. It helps to imagine

another brand approaching it legitimately in the opposite way. (The 'not like this' examples do not need to reflect just one brand.) Only then will this guidance help build your brand and be meaningful to the poor writers who have to execute it. Not too many descriptions... no more than 5. It can help to state it as an inspiring theme – it has to be memorable!

Worked example for Pizza United

When the kids are happy, everyone is happy

CREATES JOYFUL TOGETHERNESS

A class act, in a class of our own

Would speak like this...	....and not like this
Permissive. The first thought we have is YES you can.	Admonishing. 'Patrons are kindly requested....'
Convivial. We are a 'Hello everyone!' brand.....	Formal. .....not a 'Good evening, Sir' brand.
Effortlessly happy.	Serious.
Self-assured.	Innocent.

Summary:
Like a nonna, we are loving, indulgent, confident and just a little bit Italian.

Notes to the example

The full tone-of-voice guide should explain how the adjectives are connected to the brand and to the customer insight. It should also give examples of how another restaurant with a different positioning could legitimately say the same thing for that establishment. A couple of examples are given in the themes above, but the full guide would explain how it connects with the brand. In this case, the inspiring theme helps.

10. **Product DNA** Template

RIGHT TO WIN

BRAND THEME

DIFFERENTIATION

PRODUCT THEME

MANIFESTO

Guidance notes

The most relevant levers from which you build the product DNA are the right to win, and the differentiation. Others could be used if they seem particularly germane to the product or service design. The product theme is an overarching headline or ethos to guide the design, and the manifesto inspires and gives examples. A more detailed manual may well follow.

Worked example for Pizza United

RIGHT TO WIN

Fully customizable
pizza

**CREATES JOYFUL
TOGETHERNESS**

DIFFERENTIATION

A class act in
a class of its own

PRODUCT THEME

Stone-baked pizza with wholesome ingredients, fully customized
to suit every diner's needs or wants.

MANIFESTO

This is where we'd take the fussiest members of our own family.
We know stone-baked pizzas are the best, and we wouldn't put anything
on one that we wouldn't put in our own mothers' or children's mouths.
We also know how peace breaks out if the servers like kids, and are calm,
happy and sincerely wish you the best evening.

So we:
- Always have the freshest, best-quality ingredients.
- Refresh our menu as food and wines become more popular.
- Make each pizza as each customer wants it… off the menu, or bespoke,
created by customers on our iPads or with fuzzy felt, delivering an image
of their favourite pizza for our chefs to copy.
- Ensure we are on top of allergies and dietary needs, know what everything
means and what is in everything.
- We have an allergy preparation area and train our staff to the max.
- Hire people who love and are good with kids, and probably have their own.

Notes to the example

This would be expanded into detailed policy and
training manuals if it were a restaurant chain. As it
is a one-off restaurant, it probably needs no more
than an approach to staff recruitment and training,
and a fully committed chef.

Index

Picture credits

Further reading

Books I've enjoyed, learned from and applied the thinking:

David Ogilvy, *Ogilvy on Advertising*, Prion, London, 2007

D&AD, *The Copy Book*, Taschen, London, 2021

Byron Sharpe, *How Brands Grow*, Oxford University Press, Melbourne, 2010

Margaret Mark and Carol S. Pearson, *The Hero and The Outlaw: Building Extraordinary Brands Through the Power of Archetypes*, McGraw-Hill, New York, 2001

Simon Senek, *Start with Why: How Great Leaders Inspire Everyone to Take Action*, Penguin, London, 2011

Herb Sorensen, *Inside the Mind of the Shopper: The Science of Retailing*, Second Edition, Pearson, Old Tappan, 2016

Superbrands annual

CoolBrands annual

Author's acknowledgements

Thank you to the following people:

Peter Field who convinced me there was a need for a book like this in a marketing world obsessed with the latest social media platforms and digital channels. And who encouraged me to write it.

Mick Mahoney who introduced me to Liz Faber at Laurence King.

Liz and the team at Laurence King who have been patient with my innocence of how a book comes together. Thank you to the picture editor, Nick Wheldon, who supported my wish to make the book as visual as possible, which involved much hard work seeking permission from the many brands featured. And thanks to Charlie Bolton for her elegant and clever design.

Alyssa Weise, from Alygraphix, who designed the Pizza United visual assets.

Silvia Lagnado, former Global Brand Director, Dove at Unilever, for inspiring me for two decades with her Olympic vision, courage and talent.

Dana Anderson, former CMO at Mondelez for leading me and being a partner to great brand thinking and executions. And for making me laugh until snot came out of my nose.

Barbara Haase, former Global Brand Director at Vodafone for having my back and supporting the work I did there.

Everyone I worked with at two great advertising agencies: Ogilvy, who put the brand at the heart of everything and Lowe Howard-Spink, now Mullen Lowe, for whom anything short of excellence was a waste of time.

My husband, Rod Watt, who, when I needed to catch up on writing, sacrificed precious time together at evenings, weekends and holidays with good grace and good food.

Thank you to the wonderful brands and people who helped us with their stories, unearthed the pictures we needed and gave their kind permission to use their images:

Cadbury Dairy Milk, Clipper Tea, Duolingo, Isle of Harris Gin, Land Rover, Loaf, Lush, Meituan Dianping, Method, Microsoft, Milka, SAP, Simon Sinek, Singapore Airlines.